From Fading Lines

BOOK ONE

The Civil War Era

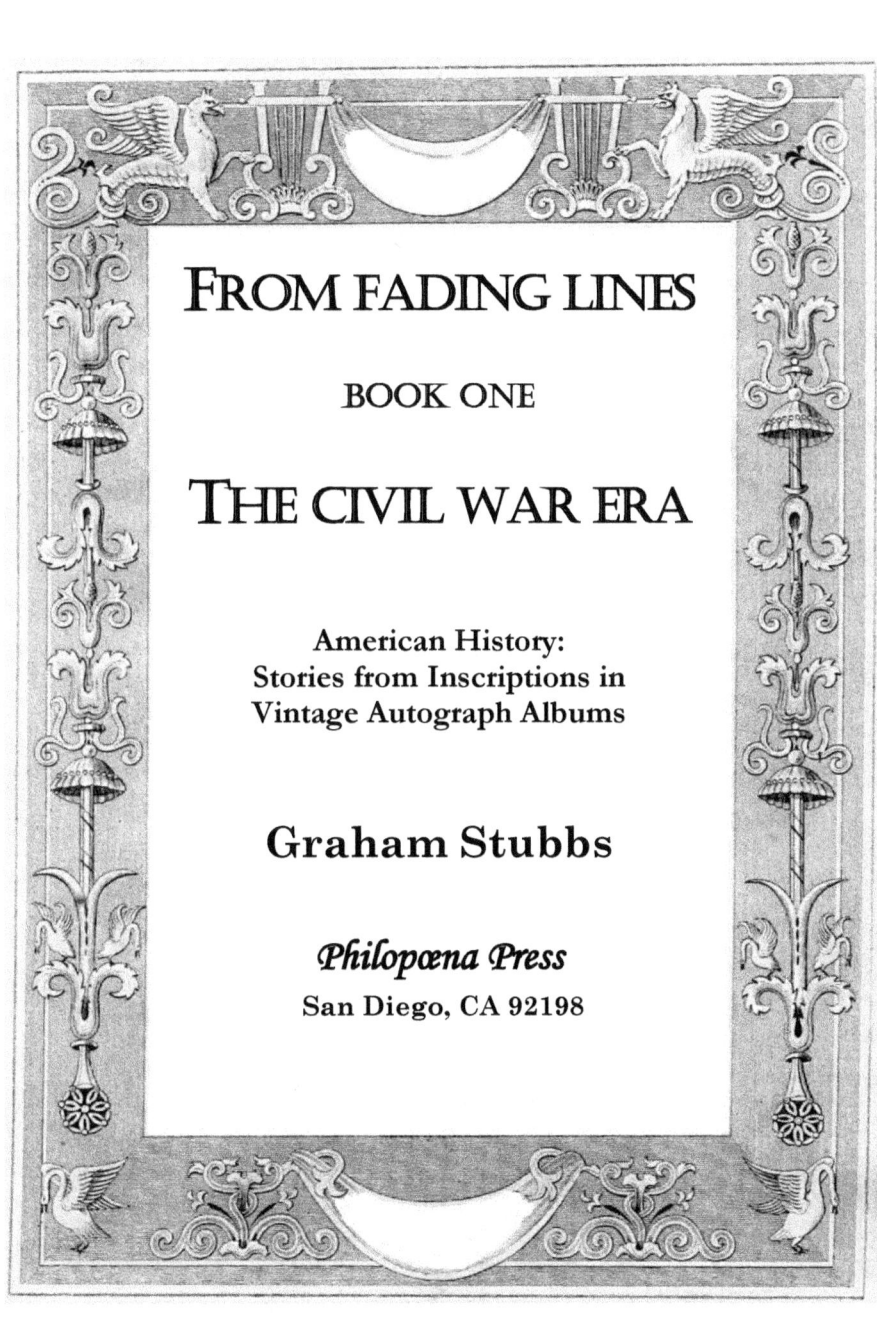

FROM FADING LINES

BOOK ONE

THE CIVIL WAR ERA

American History:
Stories from Inscriptions in
Vintage Autograph Albums

Graham Stubbs

Philopœna Press
San Diego, CA 92198

Copyright 2018 Graham S Stubbs

All rights reserved. No part of this book may be reproduced or transmitted in any form or by any means, graphic, electronic, or mechanical, including photocopying, recording, or by any information storage or retrieval system, without the express written permission of the author, except where permitted by law.

Library of Congress Control Number: 2017962717

ISBN   978-0-9996545-0-7

Printing: July 2018

Philopœna Press, of San Diego, CA specializes in studies of early autograph albums and similar handwritten books.

For more in the series *From Fading Lines* see
www.fromfadinglines.com

Albums shown in the photographs in this book are from the author's collection.

My Album's open, come and see
  What! Won't you waste a thought on me?
Write but a word, or two, or three
  And make me love to think of thee.

  John Barclay Fassitt

  Inscribed in his own album,
  Mount Holly, New Jersey, 1850

Thanks sweet girl for this proffer'd treasure
  This leaf from thy book thou'st reserved unto me
Where Fancy, unfettered, mayest wander at pleasure
  In frolicsome mood, unconditionally free ...

  Edwin B. Scarborough

  Inscribed in the album of his fiancée,
  Martha Rowe, Brownsville, Texas, 1856

ACKNOWLEDGEMENTS

My friend and neighbor Dr. Norman Magid introduced me to the Wordsmiths writers' group in Rancho Bernardo, California, where I learned how to enjoy creating the written word. My thanks go to Betty McElhatten and all the members of the Wordsmiths for their patience in listening to my stories and for their encouragement and coaching. Dr. Frank Primiano helped greatly with editing and style. Members of the Civil War Round Table of San Diego have been helpful with their counsel; in particular Ed Piper. For discussions about albums, as antiquarian books, I'm indebted to Cornelia King of the Library Company, Philadelphia, Elizabeth Watts Pope of the American Antiquarian Society, Worcester, Massachusetts, and, for a better understanding of book bindings, to Steve Beare.

The stories herein rely greatly upon family history research and I'm grateful to all the family historians who provide the results of their own research to Ancestry.com and to other genealogical websites. Wikipedia has been at least a starting point for some historical facts, and I'm indebted to the many individuals who contribute to and edit its ever-growing store of information.

Without the advice and forbearance of my wife Stephanie, who has listened to uncounted repetitions of essays, this volume would not have taken form.

At the Boys' Grammar School in my home-town Hitchin, England, our teachers drummed into us pupils the need to listen carefully to the sound of our own written words and to take responsibility for their content. With that said, I am solely accountable for any mis-statements or errors of fact in this book.

CONTENTS

Note: The story told in each chapter was prompted by researching information found in a vintage autograph album. In this table, the name of the original owner is listed together with the owner's state of residence and the year of the first entry in the album.

INTRODUCTION 1

1. THE TEXAS STATE SENATOR 3
Martha's husband was a publisher and State legislator, prior to Texas' entry into the Civil War. His murder was never solved.
Martha Rowe, Texas 1855

2. CAMP MANSFIELD 15
Samuel Hatfield, cousin of the album's owner, trained at Camp Mansfield, CT. and served in the Union Army's Heavy Artillery.
Pierre Hurlbut, Massachusetts 1861

3. POTTERS, APOTHECARIES & THE CRINOLINE CAPER 25
Monnie's pharmacist brothers were said to have helped Southern sympathizers attempt to smuggle quinine from Alexandria.
Monnie Milburn, Virginia 1865

4. GETTYSBURG 37
The boy who passed his album around to his classmates was later a Medal of Honor recipient for bravery at Gettysburg.
John Fassitt, New Jersey 1850

5. **THE AGE OF CONFEDERATE INDEPENDENCE**   55
Entries in Harriett's "Confessions" album reflect the Confederate cause. Her father was Southern humorist "Bill Arp".
Harriett Smith, Georgia 1872

6. **UNION OFFICER & VIGILANTE**   65
Maude's stepfather, a former Union officer, helped found the "Baldknobbers" post-war vigilante group.
Maude King, Missouri 1899

7. **THE MEMPHIS LEGION**   77
The position of Sarah's husband as an officer in the Memphis City militia helped him to avoid active military duty; he died from yellow fever.
Sarah Forster, Mississippi 1837

8. **VERSES FOR SONS AND BROTHERS**   91
With three brothers enlisted in the Union Army, Lydia used her album as a repository for newspaper clippings of patriotic poetry.
Lydia Rise, Pennsylvania 1858

9. **THE SOUTHERN MARSEILLAISE**   107
Handwritten in a Commonplace Book is a War-Song for the Confederacy, adapted from the French anthem, La Marseillaise.
Vernon Rhodes, Tennessee 1838

10. **THE SEED CORN OF THE CONFEDERACY**   119
Newspaper obituaries of Ella's cousins include one of the boy-soldiers recruited by the Confederacy in the last year of the war.
Ella McQueen, North Carolina 1857

11. **THE IMMORTAL SIX HUNDRED**   131
Mollie's husband and his fellow Confederate officer prisoners of war were used as human shields.
Mollie Carter, Virginia 1859

12. THE PIONEER BRIGADE — 141
The father of the album's owner commanded a company of the Union Army's Pioneer Brigade at the Battle of Stones River, Tennessee.

Bessie Brazee, Illinois 1878

13. THE LAST CAMPAIGN — 149
Lillie's two brothers went to war; the journal of the younger sibling recounted the deeds of the older man during the final Union campaign.

Lillie Gilpin, Indiana 1861

14. A SOLDIER'S THIRD WAR — 165
Lizzie's future husband, together with his uncle and his father served in the Union Army. The soldier was later called for service in the Phillipines during the Spanish American War and its successor.

Lizzie Alton, New Hampshire 1867

15. PROFESSOR GARDINER GOES TO WASHINGTON — 175
A New York inventor, father of the album's owner, witnessed one of the most momentous events in American history.

Ada F. Gardiner, Washington D.C. 1878

16. POOR BOY — 191
The CSA veteran-cousin of the girls' father committed a notorious murder that prompted the writing of a well-known American folk song.

Mary L. & Alma Dula, North Carolina 1889

BIBLIOGRAPHY — 201

INDEX — 205

APPENDIX: MORE ABOUT AUTOGRAPH ALBUMS — 213

THE AUTHOR — 219

INTRODUCTION

On a sunny June day in the year 1861, a fourteen-year-old boy walked along the rows of Union Army tents in the meadows beside the Connecticut River north of Hartford. For barely three weeks the temporary Camp Mansfield had been home to a thousand young men, who were training to become the first-in-the-nation regiment responding to President Lincoln's call for troops to serve three-year terms. Many, including the boy's cousin Samuel Hatfield, were college students. The youngster asked for inscriptions in his autograph book from soldiers who, three days hence, were due to strike their tents and depart by steamer to go to Washington and to war.

A month earlier, in an enclave of North Carolina settled mostly by Scottish immigrants, Ella McQueen bid farewell to the first of her cousins who was entering into the service of the Confederate States Army. In the following months and years one after another of her relatives departed for military duty, and she awaited reports in the newspapers about their progress. In May of 1864, it was a sad young woman who pasted into her "Boudoir Album" clippings detailing the recent deaths of three of her soldier-cousins, the youngest of whom was just seventeen years old.

These and the other stories included in this book emerged from research into old autograph albums. From fading lines that kept alive the memories of schoolmates, friends and relatives, appeared inscriptions, with names, dates and places that connect the reader to individuals who lived through the Civil War era. The original owners of the albums were mostly mothers, wives, daughters and cousins of the subjects of the stories.

Whether their names were recorded in albums before, during or after the War, these Americans all experienced that terrible event in one way or another. For this book I selected equal numbers of narratives from North and South. Whereas a majority of the subject individuals were soldiers, there were also pharmacists, merchants, politicians and an inventor, all of whom were embroiled in the conflict.

A note about what this book is not. This is not a collection of signatures of famous generals. It doesn't provide new insights into well-known campaigns. I make no pretense to be a Civil War buff or a professional historian. Rather I have identified families and individuals whose Civil War-era stories deserve to be told.

The chapter endnotes include details about each of the albums as well as historical and genealogical references.

For more about the history and evolution of autograph albums, a description of the album collection and the process of exploration which yielded the stories recorded here, see the appendix to this book.

CHAPTER 1
THE TEXAS STATE SENATOR

Tintype Photo from
MARTHA ROWE'S album 1855

In the year 1861, Texas State Senator, Edwin B. Scarborough, was one of the signatories to his state's "Declaration of Secession" from the Union. Within the year he was murdered. The above photograph is among the pages of the album that he gave in 1855 to his future wife, Martha Rowe. He inscribed the title page (overleaf) with his initials.

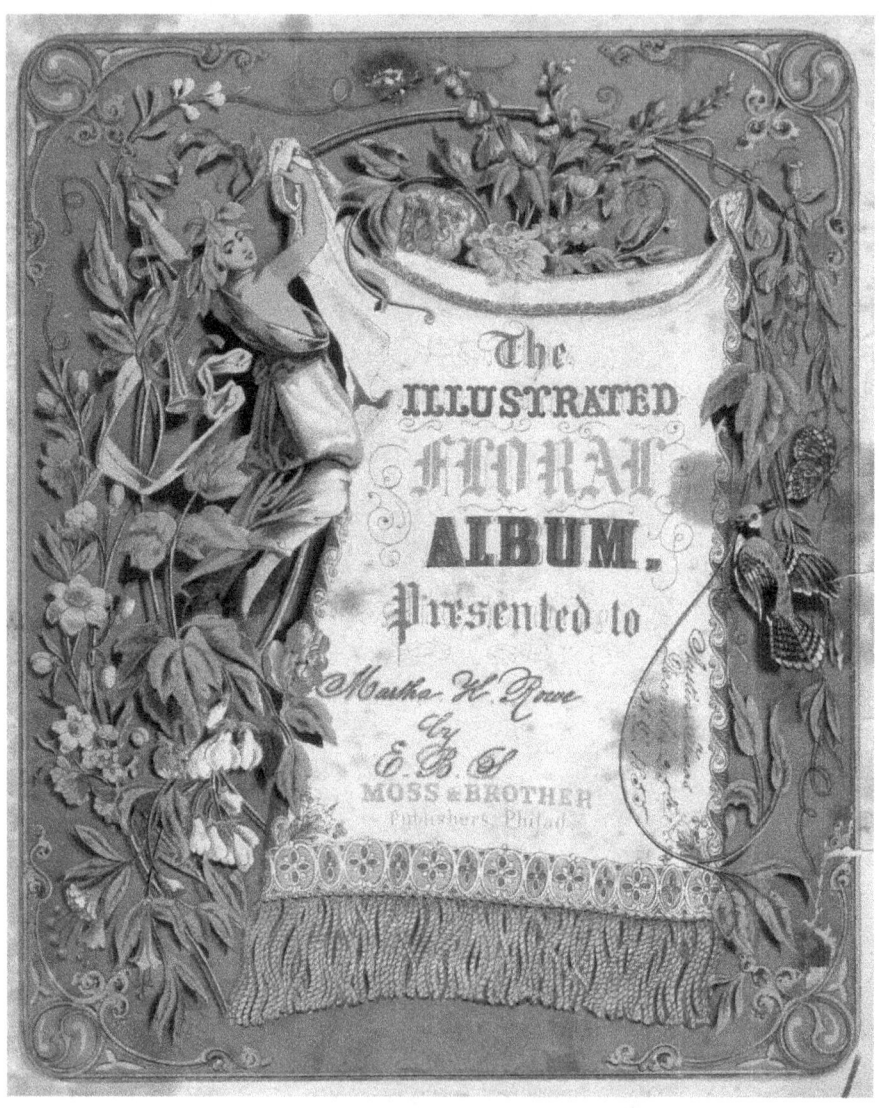

Title page of MARTHA ROWE'S album 1855,
inscribed to Martha K. Rowe by E.B.S
(Edwin B. Scarborough)

EDWIN B. SCARBOROUGH

The year 1845 had seen the resolution of the Mexican War and the annexation of Texas as an American state. Four years later, in Brownsville, a new settlement in the southernmost corner of Texas, a young printer from Georgia purchased the *American Flag*, a newspaper that took strong positions on local politics. Edwin B. Scarborough, who seems to have been something of a political firebrand, incurred much official displeasure when he used the newspaper to advocate a separate territorial status for the Nueces strip, a thirty-five mile swath of land just north of the Rio Grande.

In 1853, Scarborough at age thirty was elected State Senator for Cameron County, which included Brownsville. The Texas legislative sessions required the senator to spend the months of November through February in Austin, the state capital, and three hundred & fifty miles distant from his home district.

MARTHA ROWE[1]

Living in Austin in the 1850s was a young woman named Martha Rowe, daughter of a physician from North Carolina, Joseph Rowe. Two decades earlier, her father migrated to Texas stopping first in Tennessee, and then in Indiana where, in 1832, Martha was born. The Rowes stayed briefly in San Augustine, in the eastern part of what was then the independent Republic of Texas. Along the way from North Carolina, the doctor buried two wives. By 1838 he had moved to Austin where he married for the third time and settled.

At the age of twenty-three, Martha met Edwin, the young State Senator and publisher from Brownsville. For Christmas of 1855 he gave her the best autograph album[2] that money could buy, grander than any other on the market. With leaves measuring 11 x 8 ½ inches, Martha's album was twice as large as those of many other books of the kind. Its pastel-tinted blank pages were interleaved with hand-colored illustrations of flowers.

Front cover of MARTHA ROWE'S album 1855,

Made by the Moss & Brother Publishing Company of Philadelphia, the album was provided with a polished black lacquer cover that was decorated with floral paintings, and inset with mother of pearl.

Scarborough wrote this poem, in the flowery style of the times, in response to Martha's invitation:

To Miss M__K__R__
Thanks, sweet girl, for this proffer'd treasure
This leaf from thy book thou'st reserved unto me
Where Fancy, unfettered, mayest wander at pleasure
In frolicsome mood, unconditionally free....
EBS of Brownsville, Texas
Austin, Jan 3, 1856

The senator continued the three-verse poem in which he declared his love for the girl whom he intended to marry.

I accept with delight and tho' untutored by art
Feeble and pointless my musings may prove
Yet doubt not the motive - it springs from the heart
Unbidden it comes it is prompted by love.

Yes, thou art fair as my own sunny land,
And pure as the flowers the honey-bee sips,
Gay as the bird whose bright winglets fanned
The dew from the rose ere 'twas kissed by its lips.
Sportive as the fawn in its own fragrant wood,
Sparkling as the stars in the balmiest weather,
Mild as the Christian when prompted to good,
And joyous as that moon when the stars sang together.

I know that the muse with rich thoughts will inspire
Full many a bard in thy praises to sing
But with one there is written in letters of fire
A passion more fervent than poet can bring.
A feeling as lasting as grim visaged Time
Who heeds not the change the centuries move,
A passion as warm as that same sunny clime
Which I hail as my home: that passion is Love.

On Feb 7th, 1856 their marriage was recorded in Austin, Travis County[3], Texas. A friend of the couple wrote a five-verse poem to Scarborough, of which the first and last verses are quoted here. (The writer uses the Victorian expression "bark," a term for a sailing ship, and employed to refer to a marriage):

Thou art married, Edwin my friend,
To a fair young happy bride,
To assist thy bark to steer,
Adown life's wayward tide!

And years from now, oh! May we find,
The happy bark still gliding,
And not one chilling misty wind,
Upon its bright sails riding.

Martha was not to have many years in which to attend to her album, and the good wishes of the poet turned out to be of no avail. The year following their marriage, a son, Edwin R. Scarborough, was born to Edwin and Martha. Within another year, however, tragedy struck. Following a protracted illness, Martha died.

Tucked between the pages of the album was a newspaper clipping from the Texas State Gazette, published in Austin),, which printed this excerpt from the Brownsville newspaper. In it, Scarborough refers to his wife's death and his own return to work.

DEATH OF A WIFE.—The editor of this paper has again taken his position at the case and in the sanctum, though with a heart far less buoyant than when he left it for the sick bed of his afflicted wife, three months ago. That sweet companion and sharer of his toils and his pleasures, has been called away, and is, we cannot doubt, a seraph guest in the bright mansions of her maker.—*Brownsville Flag.*

We clip the above from the columns of our cotemporary. We know well the brief history of his matrimonial career. A sweeter woman, and more lovely union of hearts we have never seen. We have heard how steadfastly he continued to minister to her at her sick bed, when the physicians had exhausted their skill. When the hand of death deals heavily with such devotion, no one can witness it without realizing some of its mournful sadness.—*State Gazette.*

The voice of mourning never ceases. From some hill, valley or plain; in the city's mansion or from the country cottage, the sad depressing lamentation for the dead, rises, unheeded by the many. In many hearts, the desolation is but brief, and new flowers attract the admiration of the survivor, and usurp the place of the departed. There are cases however, otherwise; in which the feeling of woe is intense and enduring, and absorbs the whole nature of the bereaved. We never see one of these instances that our feelings do not glow in sympathetic response. And so, we tender to our editorial brother—a stranger though he be—the expression of our heart felt condolence.

TEXAS & THE AMERICAN CIVIL WAR

After Martha's death, the senator continued to work hard in Austin. In February 1861, the Texas legislature, by a vote of 166 to 8, adopted an Ordinance of Secession[4], which was one of a series of events that led Texas into the Confederacy and the American Civil War. The document reads in part:

> *A declaration of the causes which impel the State of Texas to secede from the Federal Union.*
>
> *The government of the United States, by certain joint resolutions, bearing the date the 1st day of March [sic], in the year A. D. 1845, proposed to the Republic of Texas, then a free, sovereign and independent nation, the annexation of the latter to the former, as one of the co-equal States thereof. ...*
> *Texas abandoned her separate national existence and consented to become one of the Confederated States ... She was received as a commonwealth holding, maintaining and protecting the institution known as negro slavery--the servitude of the African to the white race within her limits--a relation that had existed from the first settlement of her wilderness by the white race ....*
> *Her institutions and geographical position established the strongest ties between her and other slave-holding States of the confederacy.*
> *The Federal Government ... has for years almost entirely failed to protect the lives and property of the people of Texas against the Indian savages on our border, and more recently against the murderous forays of banditti from the neighboring territory of Mexico; and when our State government has expended large amounts for such purpose, the Federal Government has refused reimbursement therefor [sic], thus rendering our condition more insecure and harassing than it was during the existence of the Republic of Texas.*
> *We the delegates of the people of Texas, in Convention assembled, have passed an ordinance dissolving all political connection with the government of the United States of America.*

Edwin B. Scarborough was one of the signatories. The role of Texas in the Civil War was in fact to be primarily a supplier of troops (some 70,000 served in the Confederate States Army) and as a route for trans-shipment of supplies across the Mexican border.

The records of the Ninth Texas Legislature[5], which began in November 1861, list Scarborough as one of the two most senior members, holding the seat since 1853. In a list of changes in membership made during the session are the names of five men who resigned to join the Confederate States Army. However, regarding Edwin R. Scarborough, these words appear, "Scarborough was murdered on 7 October 1862".

ASSASSINATION

On Monday October 20th, 1862, The Semi-Weekly News of San Antonio, TX carried this report, forwarded from *The Fort Brown Flag*, the newspaper once published by Scarborough:

> **Assassination of Senator Scarborough**
> --- On Wednesday morning the people of Brownsville were under a cloud of gloom by the announcement that the Hon. Edwin B. Scarborough has been assassinated while travelling from his residence in Cameron County to the house of the Hon. E. Dougherty a distance of perhaps seven miles. He was shot in the back, the ball entering near the spine and passing out through the left breast. Senator Scarborough was riding in his ambulance[6] at the time, as traces of blood are perceptible inside the vehicle, and it appears that his horses took fright and ran into the woods where they became entangled. The deceased then jumped out of his carriage and walked a distance of 500 yards, when he fell and expired. This probably occurred about 2 P.M. as the deceased left home at 1 P.M. His body was

discovered by two soldiers who despatched it to Brownsville in charge of some neighbors.

The newspaper account finishes with:

> This atrocious assassination is entirely enveloped in mystery. He was too well known to be mistaken for a stranger traveling with money; and as he has been a consistent friend to the Mexicans, it is difficult to trace his murder to their enmity to the Americans. The only solution of the crime that the public mind has originated, accuses a Mexican named Luis Garcia, between whom and the deceased there existed a dispute about some land and the crops upon it. Garcia has been arrested. --- *Fort Brown Flag*

The public record has no more to say about the State Senator's demise, or the fate of Garcia. However, regarding the couple's child, the 1860 US Census[7] lists E.B. Scarborough, widower age 39, with his son E.R. Scarborough, age three. Nothing else is recorded as to what happened to the boy, following his father's death when Edwin (middle initial R.) was five years old. Perhaps he was adopted locally and changed his name; possibly he too met an early end. A clue was lying within the pages of the book, in the form of a scrap of carbon paper (carbon paper came into widespread use by the late 1860s after typewriters were invented); handwritten on one side is the name Edwin (middle initial R) Scarborough. It seems that something of Edwin junior survived in this album long after his parents were dead.

Martha Rowe's autograph book has no more than half a dozen handwritten entries, all signed at Austin, when Edwin most likely was attending legislative sessions. Most intriguing is the photograph shown at the beginning of this story, a tinted tintype of a man with a bold striped bow tie; with it is a lock of hair. The style of the picture and the apparent age of the subject would both be correct for it to be Edwin Scarborough.

In addition to the newspaper clippings and letters found in the album, were three hand-made visiting cards. In microscopic writing are the names of Dolores, Refugia and Rosa Santos Coy Trevino. The 1860 United States Census[8] for Brownsville lists the Trevino family, including these three young ladies, then aged 27, 16 and 23, respectively. They were in the family of a wealthy Mexican merchant, Manuel Trevino, who also served as Mexican Consul in Brownsville. The house occupied by the Trevino family for a hundred years, still stands in Brownsville; it is now known as the Stillman House, named for the family for whom it was built in 1850.

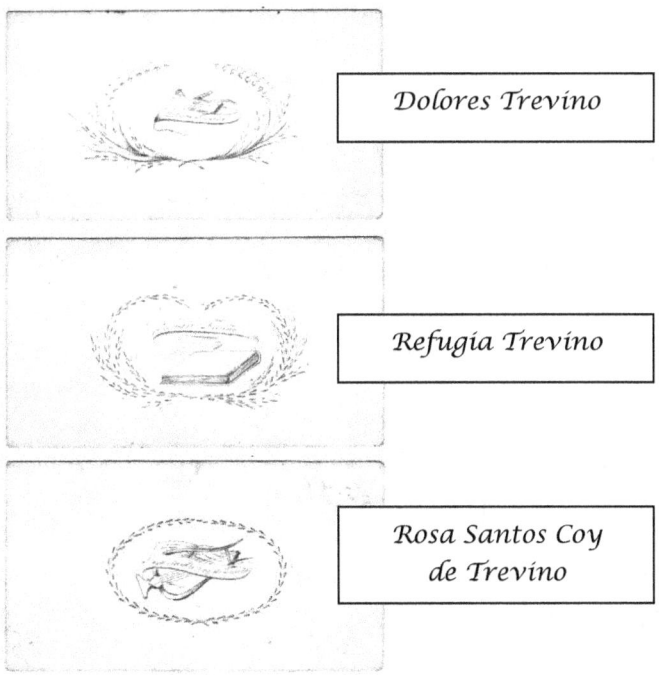

Trevino family visiting cards left between
the pages of MARTHA ROWE'S album

Why were the cards in the album? Undoubtedly, the Mexican consul was well known to the newspaper publisher.

This album yielded a tragic love story and some insight into a major chapter of American history. It also left a mystery or two yet to be solved.

Notes

[1] Ancestry.com: Ancestors of Cecil Elmo Hunt: Martha Rowe, daughter of Joseph Rowe II MD (b1802 NC d1866 Austin, Texas) and Lavinia Burditt (b1812 Tennessee, d1851).

[2] Martha Rowe's Album

Publisher:	Moss & Brother, Philadelphia
Dimensions:	11 X 8 ½ inches
Covers:	Papier-mâché, black lacquer with painted flowers over mother-of-pearl inserts
Pages:	Pastel leafs, some with color lithograph floral illustrations.
First entry:	1855

[3] FamilySearch.org: IGI Individual record for Edwin B. Scarborough and his spouse Martha K. Rowe.

[4] Texas Ordinance of Secession (February 2, 1861).

[5] Wikipedia: Ninth Texas Legislature November 4, 1861 to March 7, 1862.

[6] The significance of the word "ambulance" is unclear.

[7] Ancestry.com: US Census 1860, Brownsville Texas, E.B. Scarborough.

[8] Ancestry.com: US Census 1860, Brownsville Ward 3, Cameron County, Texas. Trevino family: head of family Manuel Trevino;; merchant; birthplace, Mexico; personal estate, $20,000. Dolores, Rosa Santos Coy and Refugia Trevino were also listed at the same location, probably the "Stillman House," occupied by the Trevino family for 100 years from 1858 (Historic American Buildings Survey, US Dept. of the Interior, Heritage Conservation & Recreation Service, HABS, Report): Manuel Santos Coy de Trevino was the Mexican Consul in Brownsville from the 1860s onwards.

CHAPTER 2
CAMP MANSFIELD

From PIERRE HURLBUT'S album 1861

The autograph album of the fourteen-year-old boy Pierre Proal Hurlbut, contains inscriptions from young soldiers in Hartford, Connecticut, who were preparing to go to war. They had been assembled at the temporary Camp Mansfield for basic training with the 4th Connecticut Volunteers Regiment and were about to depart by steamboat for Washington D.C. On that day, June 7th 1861, Pierre was excited, walking among the recruits, volunteers from his cousin's college, Wesleyan University. As he requested entries for his autograph book, the boy must have wished that he were going too!

One of the signatures was that of the boy's cousin, Samuel Proal Hatfield.

PIERRE HURLBUT'S album 1861

From PIERRE HURLBUT'S album 1861

In the spring of 1861, the young Hurlbut, whose home was in Middletown, Connecticut, attended the Wesleyan Academy, a preparatory school in Wilbraham, Massachusetts. The Academy took pride in preparing students for Wesleyan University in Middletown, where Pierre's cousin was a member of the Class of 1862. The Civil War changed everything for both of them.

The boy's autograph book[1] contains signatures only from the year 1861. Some entries are from Pierre's schoolmates at the Academy in Massachusetts. Other signatures from Camp Mansfield were of additional Wesleyan University students, each indicating that he was a member of Company "G" of the 4th Connecticut Volunteers. Still others show just "Wesleyan University, Middletown, CT" with a signature.

THE FOURTH CONNECTICUT VOLUNTEERS

June 7th 1861, when the older cousin signed the young man's book "Samuel P. Hatfield, Camp Mansfield, Hartford, Company G, 4th Regt. CV", was three days before the camp was dismantled and the soldiers embarked for what would be four years of war.

In the very first days of the American Civil War, President Lincoln on April 15th, 1861[2], thinking of it as a short-term emergency, called for seventy-five thousand men to be provided from states' militias for a period of three months. In answer to the call, volunteers in Hartford Connecticut had erected, within a month, the training tent encampment Camp Mansfield.

Thirty years later, Hatfield was called upon to write a Regimental History[3]. His written account detailed the scene in Hartford, when he was a twenty-four-year-old Corporal ready to go to war, and his fourteen-year-old cousin Pierre brought the autograph book along, hoping to meet some of the soldiers:

> *During the winter of **1860-61**, the continued threats from the Southern States were followed by real preparations for war.*

Each day some new declaration or act indicated deadly earnestness in the intention to break up our Union. Meetings were everywhere held, rolls prepared, and many signed. Comrades, you remember how you sought the eye of your neighbor and asked. "Will you go?" and the low answering "Yes" and the clasp of his hand created a new bond. We had then no thoughts of bounties, and but few were scheming for positions. To be a private in the ranks was enough. Thus we gathered, men representing nearly all occupations. Perhaps they made a squad in a village, or joined the nearest militia company in the city. How calmly we began to learn the rudiments of drill! Thus we waited and watched for the act of war that, we well knew, was to call us into real ranks. When the rebel batteries proclaimed war, these waiting men formed lines, and offered companies to the State, even before President Lincoln's first Proclamation for 75,000 men [for three months] was officially received. We can well remember our misgivings, as we thought of how small our State was and its quota would be small. Then how sadly we received notice that we could not be assigned, as the quota was complete. Yet we drilled, organized, and hoped, until the call of May 3, 1861, for 42,000 men for three years or "during the war" found us ready and the new offering was so quickly made, that the State of Connecticut had the honor of making the first report to the Government of a regiment ready; it was our regiment, the 4th Connecticut Volunteers.

About the middle of May the companies were called to rendezvous at Hartford. As they came they were quartered in churches, halls, or temporary barracks, until Camp Mansfield was formed at the corner of Windsor Avenue and Fish-Fry Streets. At first, before the Commissary Department was organized, we were fed by contract in hotels and restaurants.

By this time the entire inadequacy of the three-months troops became apparent, and the following dispatch was sent to the Governors of Connecticut, Maine, Michigan, New Hampshire, New Jersey, and Wisconsin.

WAR DEPARTMENT, June 3, 1861.
To Gov. Buckingham. NORWICH, CONN.
Send on to this place your three years regiments as soon as organized. Report when.
SIMON CAMERON, Secretary of War.

This dispatch hastened the preparations for our departure, which was fixed for June 10, 1861, when we were to start for the front. On Monday morning early, all was bustle and preparation. The tents were ordered to be struck at eight o'clock, and rumor was that we were to proceed immediately to Washington by way of Baltimore. Accordingly, as the city clocks struck eight, at the tap of the drum, the tents fell; Camp Mansfield was no more; and by another hour a long line of army wagons, loaded with camp equipage, was coming down the meadow road to the steamboat dock for shipment. At last, after marching about town, and being overwhelmed with heat, and hand-shakings, and hurrahs, and bouquets, and waving handkerchiefs, and crying ladies, and smiling ladies, and enthusiastic men, who wanted to shake you all to pieces in bidding you good bye, we succeeded in getting safely embarked, about 4 o'clock P. M., on the steamboats City of Hartford and Granite State.

From fifteen to twenty thousand people were assembled to witness our departure. All the buildings and docks in sight were thronged with spectators. The steamboat wharf was covered with a dense and suffocating crowd.

There was music, and firing of cannon, and cheering, and waving of hats and handkerchiefs on all sides, and, as we steamed down the river, new crowds and new cannon, new hats and new handkerchiefs, and new fresh cheers, until the reciprocating ones on board became utterly tired out. Fortunately, night threw her veil around the steamers and left the wearied soldiers to repose."

The Regimental History goes on to describe the transformation of the regiment's role, and the change of its name from 4th Connecticut Volunteers, Infantry to 1st Connecticut Heavy Artillery. The volume, copiously illustrated with maps and photographs, details the regimental history and campaigns, through the final siege and fall of Petersburg and of Richmond.

SAMUEL P. HATFIELD

Cousins Samuel Hatfield and Pierre Hurlbut had been raised in the same home almost as brothers. Samuel's mother had died soon after he was born, and his father, Wyatt Hatfield, sent the child to live with his mother's sister and her wealthy husband, Samuel Hurlbut. Even after his father remarried and there were more children, the young Samuel Hatfield remained with his aunt and uncle. The US Census for 1850[4] had the boy living with Hurlbuts and with their family name. Ten years later[5], the census listed him as Samuel P Hatfield, age 23, occupation student. At the same dwelling, his cousin Pierre Proal Hurlbut, named for a French ancestor of his mother Evelina Proal, is listed at fourteen years of age.

The records show that Corporal Hatfield progressed rapidly through the ranks[6]. In December 1861 he was promoted to Sergeant. Two months later, while the regiment was attached to the defenses of Washington, D.C., he was made second lieutenant, and two weeks after that first lieutenant; he was promoted to captain in January 1864. Close to the end of the War, following the siege of Petersburg, in May 1865 he was appointed to the rank of major, assigned to the field and staff. He was mustered out in Washington, D.C. in September 1865.

PIERRE HURLBUT

The young Pierre Hurlbut, had desperately wanted to serve in the Union Army but was restricted by his age. Initially, most men entering the Army were twenty years old or older; the hard lower limit was eighteen years of age. However, as manpower shortages occurred, some exceptions were allowed for certain occupations. The records for the 14th Connecticut Infantry[7] show Pierre, then age sixteen, enlisted as a musician on the 31st of July 1862. Six months later, he received a disability discharge.

The determined young man enlisted again in May 1864, this time for one of the most dangerous branches of the army, the Signal Corps. The duties of the Signal Corps included spotting the enemy, point-to-point communication, and interception of enemy signals. In many instances, this required occupying positions in tall trees or on purpose-built wooden towers[8]. (See illustration on page 22).

Sense of duty, necessity of exposure to fire, and importance of mission were conditions incompatible with personal safety and many of the men of the Signal Corps paid the price. The ratio in the Signal Corps of those killed to those wounded was one hundred & fifty per cent, as against twenty per cent in regular units.

For much of the war, the Union Army had troops occupying parts of Eastern Virginia and the northeast corner of North Carolina, an area that controlled the entrance from the Atlantic Ocean to the James River, which flowed past the Confederate capital, Richmond. In 1863, troops raised from these occupied territories were combined to form the Army of the James, and it was to this army that Hurlbut was assigned.

In April 1865, the young Signal Corps soldier was among these troops who were present when Confederate General Robert E. Lee surrendered the Army of Northern Virginia to General Ulysses S. Grant at Appomattox Courthouse, Virginia. Pierre Hurlbut was discharged from there in July 1865.

Signal Tower at Appamattox River
December 1864

AFTER THE CIVIL WAR

Subsequent to the War, each man found outlets for the organizational skills learned during military service.

In 1892, in recognition of his experiences throughout the entire war, Samuel Hatfield was asked to research and write the history[3] of his regiment. In 1915, Hatfield presented to the library of Wesleyan University many of the original photographs taken under his direction during the course of the war. In his cover letter[9] he gave credit to students from Wesleyan, many of whom formed Company G of the Regiment.

> *It is desired to be of the record that, of the students thus engaged, at the last, in the breaking of the line at Fort Mahone, Petersburg, April 2nd 1865, the University was actively represented and the supply of ammunition maintained through the day. By breaking the Confederate line here Richmond was evacuated that night and the Confederacy dissolved like a broken bubble. Wesleyan was part of the bayonet point that broke it up, and the Union was saved.*

Hatfield is listed in the 1900[10] US Census as a civil engineer, living in New York. He was awarded a patent[11] in 1906 for "Apparatus for laying Electrical Conductors." His invention included a plough that could bury cable below the bottom of a body of water. In 1911, as a veteran of the Civil War, Hatfield, a non-graduate of the Class of 1862, was retrospectively awarded the degree of B.A. *nunc pro tunc*[12] from Wesleyan University.

In the census for 1880[13], Pierre Hurlbut's occupation is given as a surveyor in Chattanooga, Tennessee. When he died in 1915 in Atlanta, Georgia, his obituary[14] said that he was a United States Government civil engineer and a member of the American Society of Engineering Contractors.

Notes:

[1] Pierre Hurlbut's Album:
>   Publisher: Rufus Merrill & Son. Concord, New Hampshire Made for the Wesleyan Academy, Wilbraham, Mass.
>   Dimensions: 6 ¾ X 4 inches
>   Covers: Leather over boards, gilt stamped AUTOGRAPHS
>   Pages: White pages, frontispiece with engraving of the Academy. Gilt edging.
>   First entry: 1861

[2] Wikipedia: President Lincoln's Proclamation April 15th, 1861, calling forth state militias.

[3] Taylor, J.C. & Hatfield, S.P. *History of the First Connecticut Artillery & of the Siege Trains of the Armies Operating against Richmond, 1862-1865.* Case, Lockwood & Brainery, Hartford, 1893.

[4] Ancestry.com: US Census 1850.

[5] Ancestry.com: US Census 1860.

[6] *Civil War Research and Genealogy Database*, Historical Datasystems Inc.: Soldier History: Samuel P. Hatfield.

[7] US National Park Service: Civil War soldier records, 14th Regiment, Connecticut Infantry, Company B; Pierre P Hurlbut, Musician.

[8] Lossing, Benson John. *The Pictorial Field Book of the Civil War in the United States of America.* (Signal tower illustration) Volume 1, Belknap, 1874.

[9] Letter held at Wesleyan University, Special Collections & Archives.

[10] Ancestry.com: US Census 1900.

[11] US Patent 815,163, Samuel P. Hatfield, March 13, 1906.

[12] The Latin phrase *nunc pro tunc* means "now for then," that is, retroactively.

[13] Ancestry.com: US Census 1880.

[14] *Engineering News*, 1914, Vol. 71, No. 15, page 816..

CHAPTER 3
POTTERS, APOTHECARIES & THE CRINOLINE CAPER

CRINOLINE AND QUININE—A DELICATE INVESTIGATION—SCENE AT THE PROVOST-MARSHAL'S, WASHINGTON—SEARCHING MRS BUCKNER FOR CONTRABAND SUPPLIES FOR THE REBELS—QUININE FOUND.—SEE PAGE 139.

Discovering contraband in the lady's crinoline

Smuggling of Confederate medical contraband in women's petticoats was widely publicized in a story that ran in northern periodicals[1] in the year 1862. The incident was linked to two pharmacists who signatures appear in their sister's autograph album[2]. They were members of the family of a celebrated potter in Alexandria, Virginia.

THE ALBUM

MONNIE MILBURN'S album 1865

The album was purchased from Alexandria bookseller Robert Bell, and presented to Monnie in 1865 by her father, Benedict C. Milburn.

*Dec 25th 1865.
A Present to
Monnie Milburn,
from her Papa.*

Monnie's teacher inscribed this unusual double acrostic, which spells out "MISS M MILBURN FROM TEACHER."

> My Best Wishes.
> [A double acrostic.]
>
> **M**y dear young friend, **F**or thee I'll make
> **I**n simple lines of **R**hyme,
> **S**ome heartfelt wishes.—**O**'er thy life
> **S**peed every **M**oment's time
> **M**id some useful work; '**T** will give
> **M**ost pleasure, **E**'en most pure,
> **I**n times when **A**ge shall come
> **L**ike Winter, **C**hill and drear.
> **B**e wise in youth, **H**old fast and strong
> **U**nto God's **E**verlasting word.
> **R**egard his law, **R**aise high thy thought
> **N**or lose what thou hast heard.
>
> Alex. Jan 14, '66

THE MILBURNS OF ALEXANDRIA

Benedict C. Milburn was born in the year 1805 in St. Mary's, Maryland, on the western shore of Chesapeake Bay. At the age of seventeen he made his way up the Potomac River to Alexandria, Virginia, to apprentice in the pottery business. In 1828 he married Thirza Coad, also from St. Mary's. The couple had three daughters and seven sons.

The first daughter, Ann, died in infancy. The second, Sarah Florence, born in 1846, married a dry goods merchant in Alexandria. Two of the sons followed their father into the pottery business, producing stoneware that is highly collectible today. Four others trained as pharmacists. Margaret Jane "Monnie" Milburn, born in 1852[3,4] was the youngest member of the family.

THE WILKES STREET POTTERY

The Milburn business was a successor to two previous potters who produced stoneware at the Wilkes Street Pottery, Alexandria. The first, starting in 1810, was John Swann, whose wares were mostly sold through a china merchant, Hugh Smith. Swann started with plain brown jugs and jars and later employed blue decoration using cobalt. Smith took over in 1825 and continued until 1841, when Milburn purchased the business. He was very successful; his brushed blue cobalt decorations became more and more elaborate. The Milburn family continued the business until the year 1876.

THE MILBURN APOTHECARIES

Four of the Milburn brothers trained as druggists (also termed pharmacists or apothecaries). At the age of 17, in 1848, the eldest, John Alexander Milburn, first entered the drug business with a local pharmacist. By 1851 he opened his own business in Alexandria. Five years later, his brother, Joseph Parker Milburn, opened a drug store, in which John was also a partner, under the famous Willard's Hotel, on Pennsylvania Avenue, in the center of Washington. A third brother, Washington Clinton Milburn, was apprenticed to the drug store business in 1860; after the Civil War he purchased his own drug store in Washington. The fourth brother, James Clinton Milburn was training as a pharmacist when he enlisted in the Confederate States Army in 1862. After the war, he operated a grocery store in Alexandria.

A page of Monnie's album with her brothers' signatures in hand-drawn rectangles, representing "visiting cards".

John A. Milburn signed "*Jno A Milburn.*"

Washington Clinton Milburn signed "*Wash'n C. Milburn.*"

James Clinton Milburn signed "*J.C. Milburn.*"

ALEXANDRIA DURING THE CIVIL WAR

The original District of Columbia, formed in 1790 for a national capital on the Potomac River, was in the shape of a square, with its corners at the four points of the compass. At that time the Federal District measured 10 miles on each side, totaling 100 square miles. The existing city of Alexandria[5] was at the southernmost corner of the square, across the Potomac and just six miles downstream from the Nation's new Capital city, Washington. In the 1830s, the

District's southern territory of Alexandria went into economic decline partly due to neglect by Congress. The city of Alexandria was a major market in the American slave trade and pro-slavery residents feared that abolitionists in Congress would end slavery in the District, further depressing the economy. Alexandria's citizens petitioned Virginia to take back the land it had donated to form the District, and in 1846, Congress agreed to return all the territory that had been ceded by Virginia. Thereafter, the District's area consisted only of the land originally donated by Maryland; the southern boundary was the Potomac River.

Thus, when the Civil War began, Washington was vulnerable to Confederate attack across the river from Virginia. The morning after May 23rd, 1861, when Virginians had voted to secede from the Union, thousands of federal troops from Washington poured into Alexandria to seize the city. During the War a string of forts was built to the west and north to afford protection to Washington from Confederate forces, which controlled the rest of Virginia. Alexandria became a busy Union supply depot. Citizens had to obtain permits to travel outside the city. Business owners had to take an oath of allegiance to the federal government in order to obtain a license to continue to operate. Those Alexandrians who had not fled lived under martial law. Southern sympathizers had plenty of opportunity to make mischief.

TWO OF THE MILBURN SONS GO TO WAR

While John and Joseph Milburn remained in Alexandria during the war, operating their pharmacy businesses, their brothers Washington and James went off to war, both seconded to the Medical Department of the Confederate States Army.

Washington C. Milburn[6] had been a member of the local "Alexandria Riflemen," Virginia Militia. He enlisted at Alexandria in the 17th Virginia Infantry, Pickett's Division of the C.S.A. on April 17th, 1861. Initially a regimental hospital nurse, he became a regimental hospital steward (equivalent of a sergeant major) for the duration of the War. His younger brother James Clinton Milburn[7], enlisted in the same regiment on May 29th 1862 at Richmond, Virginia and served as a field hospital nurse. The regiment suffered massive casualties during the conflict, but both brothers survived and were paroled at Appomattox[8] Court House, Virginia. On Wednesday April 12th, 1865, when they started their journey home, they were two of only 48 enlisted men and officers left of the more than a thousand who had been members of their regiment.

THE "QUININE AND CRINOLINE ESCAPADE"[9]

The ladies' crinoline of the mid-nineteenth century consisted of one or two petticoats worn over a lightweight steel skirt-shaped structure. It was sometimes referred to as a cage-crinoline. It was perfect for hiding contraband, and there were many Civil War stories of women smuggling anything from weapons and munitions to food and medical supplies across enemy lines.

One such lady was Louisa Berryman Buckner, daughter of a Virginia planter, and niece of Montgomery Blair, Postmaster General of the United States, and a member of President Lincoln's cabinet. In late October 1862, she embarked with two companions on a grand adventure. With her were her mother Louisa Hipkins Turner, and twenty-three year-old Marcus Buck Hobson Bayly, whose father had a mansion in Washington and a plantation in Virginia. Although they had powerful Union connections, the Buckner and Bayly family sympathies were decidedly southern.

The party traveled to Washington from Virginia ostensibly to buy food and supplies. They were confident that their high-level connections would assist them. During their visit to Washington they stayed at the home of Louisa Turner's daughter and son-in law, a naval officer, Benjamin Gallaher. The two ladies went to call upon Blair, from whom they secured a personal gift of $500, and a note certifying that they were loyal citizens of the Union, and that the goods they were carrying were for their own personal use. A similar note from President Lincoln himself attested to their good character.

While the ladies were so occupied, Bayly visited three druggists, including J.P. Milburn & Co., which was operated by Joseph Parker Milburn and his elder brother John. Bayly purchased from each of the pharmacies small quantities of medication, acquiring a total of 120 ounces of quinine, the drug used to treat malaria, which medication was in extremely short supply in the south. The motivation was profit. A virtual monopoly on the supply of the drug was held by the Philadelphia firm of Powers & Weightman, which imported the raw ingredients from Brazil. An ounce of the quinine that Bayly purchased for $5.25 sold for seventy dollars in Richmond, Virginia. The druggists also made a tidy profit; they received from Bayly twice the market value. For the return journey, Louisa Buckner had arranged to modify her crinoline skirt, with special pockets made of waterproof oiled silk in which to hide the quinine.

In the meantime, a black servant in the Gallaher household, aware of the plan to smuggle contraband medicines, alerted detective authorities of the names of the people involved and that their destination was in Virginia. The next day the party left Washington by wagon, intentionally taking a route to avoid Union pickets. When they reached the Union-controlled Fairfax, Virginia Courthouse their wagon was seized and searched, but no contraband found. They were almost at their destination when they were stopped again, and this time the crinoline was searched, the quinine discovered, and the suppliers identified. A few days later the *Washington Evening Star* newspaper reported on the affair and on the arrest of the pharmacists:

> Messrs. Kidwell of Georgetown, Peale of Alexandria and Milburn of this city were yesterday arrested and sent to Old Capitol Prison for selling these parties the contraband medicines, knowing as is alleged, where they were to be carried.

Mrs. Turner was released immediately after the arrest and allowed to continue to her home. Her daughter, Louisa, was released a few days later having signed an oath of allegiance to the Union. The young man, Buck Bayly, stayed in jail for six weeks until he too signed the oath. Ultimately the druggists were exonerated, although in fact the proprietors of all three businesses had close southern ties. Eventually, the newspaper printed a retraction, saying, "Young clerks or storeboys, only, were implicated."

THE MILBURN BROTHERS AFTER THE WAR

After the Civil War, the Milburn Pottery[10] business produced primarily undecorated jars and jugs; very little decorated stoneware was produced at the Wilkes Street location. Benedict Milburn died in April 1867, and his son Stephen took over the business for the years 1867-1871, and was succeeded by William Lewis Milburn, who ran the pottery until it closed in 1876. Milburn stoneware is nowadays highly prized by collectors; individual pots can sell for upwards of a thousand dollars.

Before he took over the pottery in 1871, William, together with his brother James Clinton Milburn, operated a grocery business in Alexandria for a number of years, with assistance from their youngest brother, Ethelbert W. Milburn. Three of the brothers, Joseph Parker, Washington C. and John A. Milburn, continued in the pharmacy business in Washington D.C. All three were active members of the American Pharmaceutical Association, as noted in their respective obituaries in 1874[11], 1891[12] and 1896[13]. The death notices of Joseph and John Milburn make it clear that they were seen as honorable members of the Washington community, and highly regarded within their profession. There is no mention in the obituaries of the crinoline and quinine affair!

"MONNIE" MILBURN, OWNER OF THE ALBUM

In 1872, Margaret Jane "Monnie" Milburn married a northern veteran of the war, Arthur P. Whitney of Saratoga, New York. He had served the New York Heavy Artillery Regiment of the Union Army. The couple met when he came to work in Washington D.C. as a US Government Clerk after the war. They had three children of whom the youngest, Paul Clinton Whitney in 1894, at the age of eleven, inscribed his mother's album with these words:

> *To mother*
> *What can make me happy here?*
> *Nothing like the love of Mother.*
> *What can drive away my fear?*
> *Nothing like the love of mother.*
> *Paul Whitney*

Three years later, Margaret Jane "Monnie" Milburn Whitney[2], passed away. She is buried in Rock Creek Cemetery, Washington, D.C.

Notes:

[1] *Frank Leslie's Magazine,* November 12, 1862
[2] Monnie Milburn's Album:
  Publisher: Leavitt & Allen, New York
  Dimensions: 8 X 6 ¼ inches
  Covers: Brown Leather over boards. Gilt-stamped "LEAVES OF FRIENDSHIP:" within a floral frame. Spine stamped "ALBUM".
  Pages: Title Page "LEAVES OF FRIENDSHIP". Pastel pages, some with engraved illustrations, gilt edged.
  First entry: 1865
[3] www.findagrave.com: memorial to Margaret Milburn Whitney. birth July 16, 1852, burial in Rock Creek Cemetery, Washington D.C:.
[4] Ancestry.com: Cutter family tree: Benedict Colbert Milburn family & life.

[5] The Washington Post: "The Federal Occupation of Alexandria in the Civil War changed and spared the city." Brady Dennis. Apr 7, 2011.

[6] www.findagrave.com: memorial to Pvt. Washington C. Milburn cites Civil War military service. Birth Dec 30, 1840 / death Aug 7, 1891.

[7] www.findagrave.com: memorial to James Clinton Milburn cites Civil War military service. Birth Jan 14, 1844 / death Sep 9, 1912.

[8] www.myheritage.com: History of 17th Virginia Infantry Regiment Company H, The Old Dominion Rifles.

[9] The story told here might have ended with the death of the album's owner, were it not for an article with the title "Crinoline and Quinine," written by William Page Johnson, II that appeared in the Fall of 2012 issue of *The Fair Facs Gazette*, Published by the Fairfax, Virginia Historical Society.

[10]: *Alexandria Stoneware: The Wilkes Street Pottery*. Alexandria Archaeology Museum

[11] Am. Jour. Pharm: May 1, 1874; obituary of J. Parker Milburn. Died Washington March 4th, 1874

[12] Proceedings of the American Pharmaceutical Association: *Report of Committee on Membership*, July 1892: Obituary of W.C. Milburn. Died August 7th, 1891.

[13] American Pharmaceutical Association: *Record 1896, Minutes of Second Session*, obituary of John A. Milburn.

CHAPTER 4
GETTYSBURG

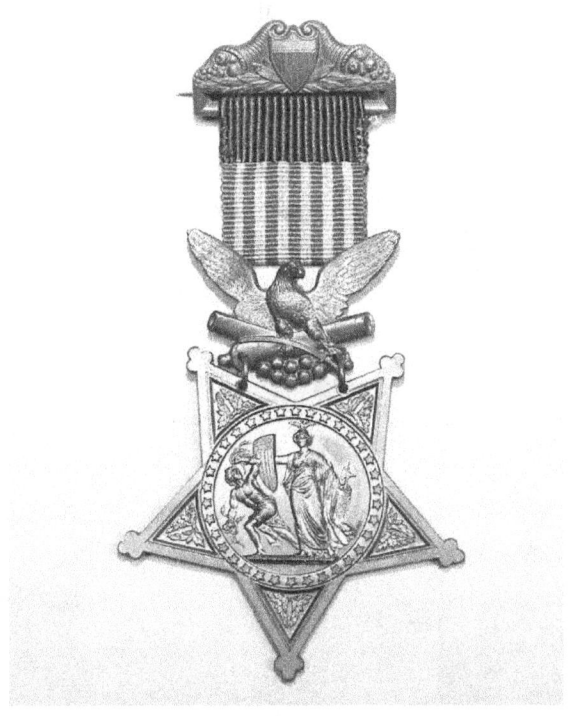

Medal of Honor
1862 – 1896 United States Army version

As a boy, John Barclay Fassitt, a future Medal of Honor recipient, kept an autograph album[1] to record inscriptions from teachers and classmates at the exclusive boarding school to which his family sent him. He and another signer of the memory book played important roles in what was arguably the most decisive battle of the Civil War, Gettysburg.

THE SCHOOLBOY & HIS ALBUM

John Barclay Fassitt came from a wealthy Philadelphia family who made their money in the dry goods merchandising business. His grandfather, James Fassitt, besides being the head of the family concern, was also chairman of the Pennsylvania Railroad Company[2]. The boy's father Alfred was additionally president of a Pennsylvania coal company. Yet, despite the family wealth, rather than use a fancy store-bought album, the boy adapted a hardcover blank notebook that once served as a duty-book in the offices of the family business.

JOHN BARCLAY FASSITT'S album 1850

He numbered each of the forty-two pages of the little book and prepared an index of names.

Attached to the inside front cover is one of its more remarkable features, a disc constructed from folded and cut paper. Lifting the center by means of an attached thread turns the paper into a cone, beneath which are revealed written on the inside cover the words "John B. Fassitt's Album." Above is written the source of the book, "James Fassitt Co., Duty Book."

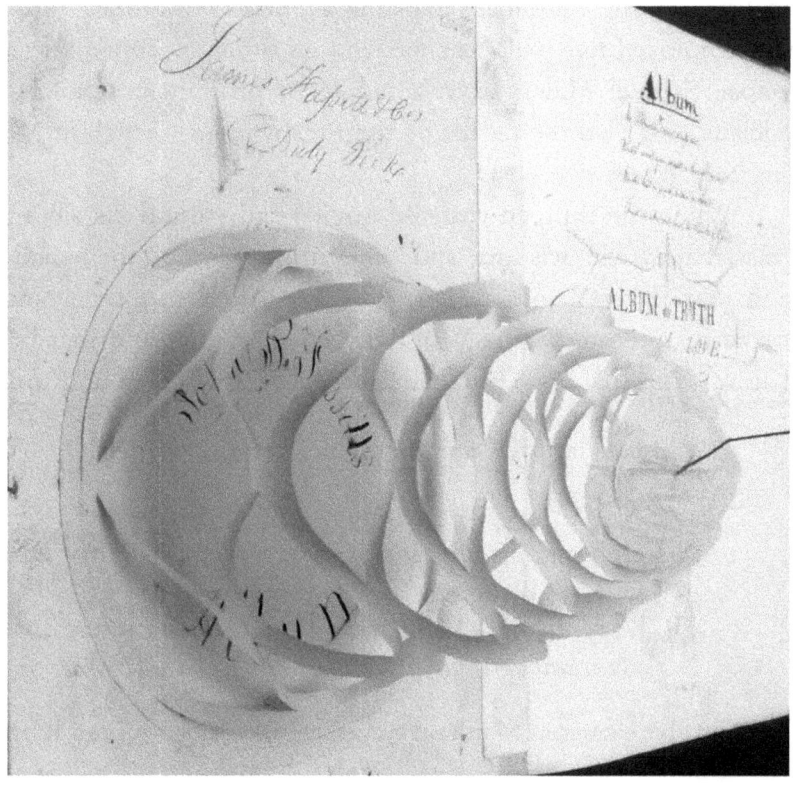

Cut-paper insert in JOHN BARCLAY FASSITT'S album

On the following page he wrote this verse:

My Album's open, come and see
What! Won't you waste a thought on me?
Write but a word, or two, or three
And make me love to think of thee.

Nineteen of his classmates provided inscriptions, as did three of the teachers. Most entries make reference to the institution's name, "West Jersey Collegiate School." Residing there in the year 1850, according to the United States Census[3], were thirty-three male students, ranging in age from ten to eighteen. In addition to twenty pupils from New Jersey or Pennsylvania, there were southern boys from Virginia, the Carolinas, Alabama, Kentucky and Maryland. The school employed five male teachers and six other staff members. The principal, Samuel Miller, from a family of prominent scholars and physicians, was also the pastor of the Presbyterian Church in Mount Holly, New Jersey.

When the thirteen-year-old boy passed around his album for his classmates' wit, wisdom and signatures, none of them had any notion that fewer than a dozen years later their country would be involved in the cataclysmic War Between the States and that Fassitt and at least three of his schoolmates would be soldiers in uniform.

Aaron Brainard Jerome, then ten years old, wrote:

Dear Johny (sic)
Be kind and affectionate and every one will love you.
When you look upon these lines
rember (sic) your friend and School Mate
September 17 1850 AD   Brainard Jerome.

Twelve-year-old Maitland Soutter, of Florida, quoted Byron:

Feb 4th 1850   Dear Fassitt

He who ascends to the mountaintops shall find
The loftiest peaks most wrapt in clouds and snows;
He who surpasses or subdues mankind,
Must look down on the hate below....
Though high above the sun of glory glows,
And far beneath the earth and ocean spread,
Round him are icy rocks, and loudly blow,

Contending tempests on his naked head,
And thus reward the toil which to those summits led.

I hope you will ever remember
Your dear Friend & Fellow Scholar
Maitland Soutter

William Henry McDonald used the words of the Scottish poet Thomas Campbell:

To John
Oh! Deep enchanting prelude to repose
The dawn of bliss the twilight of our woes.
West Jersey Collegiate school
Mount Holly N. Jersey

THE CIVIL WAR

In addition to Fassitt, three of the boys who signed of the album later went to war, Brainard Jerome, Maitland Souter and William McDonald.

The first of these to enter the military was Jerome[4] who enlisted in the First New Jersey Infantry Regiment as a first sergeant on April the 25th, 1861, thirteen days after hostilities began. He was later commissioned as an officer in the Army Signal Corps.

On May 16th, 1862 Maitland Soutter was employed as a railroad agent in Fernandina, the northernmost city in Florida, before he joined the 2nd Florida Cavalry Regiment. During the War, his Confederate Army unit was never ordered out of its home state.

William McDonald[5] enlisted on June 27th, 1862, but returned home to Pennsylvania in March 1863 following an attack of typhoid fever. He was once again drafted, but he managed to hire a substitute who took his place for the rest of the conflict.

Additionally, two brothers of the school's principal each raised a company of artillery, Dr. Elihu Spencer Miller for the Union Army and John Miller for the Confederacy.

Between leaving West Jersey Collegiate School and the outbreak of the Civil War, Fassitt had attended Harvard and worked in the family business in Philadelphia. The 30th anniversary Report of the Harvard College Class of 1858[6] includes this about John Fassitt:

> *At the breakout of the war, he was traveling in the South. He returned to Philadelphia and in April **1861**, went out with the Philadelphia City Troop of which he was a member for the three months' campaign. At its close he was mustered out and immediately remustered as second lieutenant, Company H, Twenty-third Pennsylvania Volunteers. ... Promoted first lieutenant and adjutant of his regiment July **1961**. ... Was promoted captain on the field at Malvern Hill (in July **1862**) for "gallant and meritorious service in the face of the enemy." Was in the battles of Chantilly and Fredericksburg with his regiment then returned to General Birney's staff and was in the battle of Gettysburg.*

Evidently the bravery of the one-time schoolboy from Philadelphia was recognized early.

GETTYSBURG

The Battle of Gettysburg[7] was fought July 1-3, 1863 in and around the Pennsylvania town from which it takes its name. The battle resulted in the largest number of combined casualties of the entire War, and is sometimes described as the turning point of the conflict. The battle pitted Union General George Gordon Meade's Army of the Potomac against Confederate General Robert E. Lee's Army of Northern Virginia. The outcome terminated General Lee's second attempt to invade the North, by which he had hoped to penetrate as far as Harrisburg, or Philadelphia.

Two of the Union officers close to the center of the action were Captain Fassitt and his one-time school classmate, Lt. Brainard Jerome, who had already distinguished himself[8] at the Battle of Antietam in September 1862.

Lt. Brainard Jerome (seated)
Elk Mountain signal tower, Antietam, Maryland
September 1862

FIRST DAY OF THE BATTLE OF GETTYSBURG: JULY 1ST, 1863

During the first engagements of the battle, Lieutenant Aaron Brainard Jerome, serving as a signals officer for the Union Cavalry Division, was positioned in the steeple of Gettysburg Seminary, northwest of the town, to observed and report on the Confederate troop movements.

Low ridges to the northwest of town were defended initially by Union cavalry, and soon reinforced with two corps of infantry. However, two large Confederate corps assaulted them from the northwest and north, collapsing the hastily developed Union lines, sending the defenders retreating through the streets of town to the hills just to the south. Lee's objective was to engage the Union army and destroy it.

After the war, Cavalry General Buford, writing about Jerome's talents and his contributions the Union victory at Gettysburg had this to say[9], "Lieutenant Jerome, of the signal corps, was ever on the alert, and through his intrepidity and fine glasses on more than one occasion kept me advised of the enemy's movements when no other means were available."

Lt. Brainard Jerome

Jerome was later at a signaling station on the rise known As Little Round Top, where he would also have been perfectly placed to observe the later heroic actions of his former classmate, John Fassitt.[10]

GETTYSBURG: THE SECOND DAY, JULY 2ND.

By the second day, the Union line was laid out in a defensive formation resembling an inverted fish-hook, occupying high ground to the south of the town; the longer arm of the hook was on the west side, along what was known as "Cemetery Ridge" with rise known as "Little Round Top" at the southern end. The Confederate line paralleled that of the Union soldiers about a mile west of Cemetery Ridge. Some elements of the Union Forces had overextended to the west of the line into a peach orchard, and were driven back.

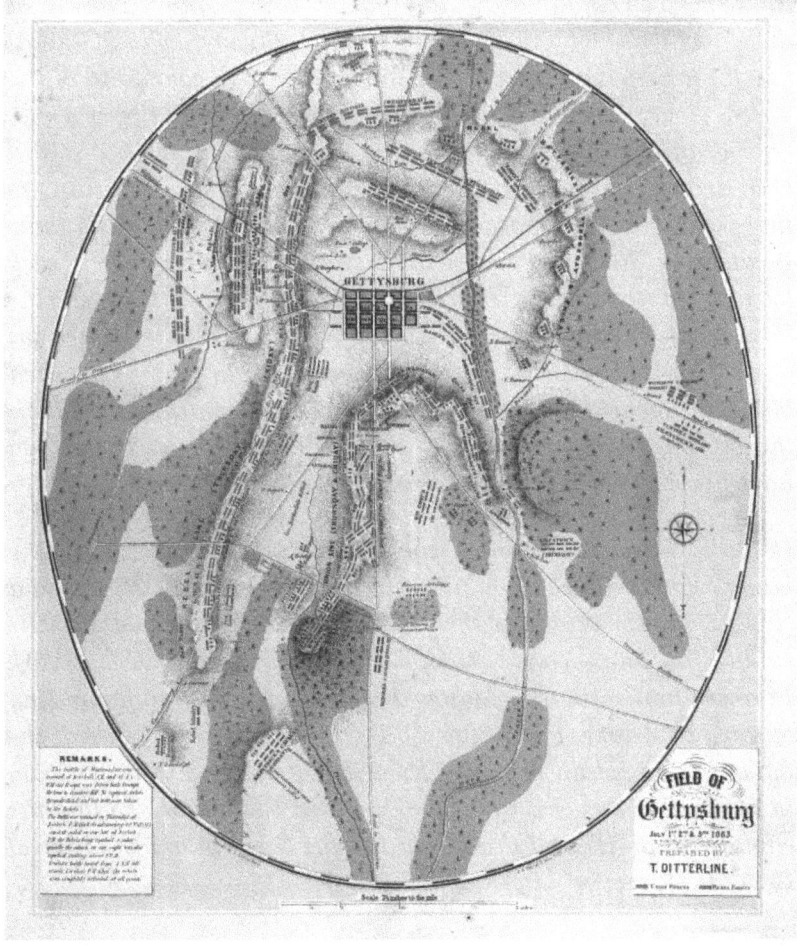

Gettysburg: Union & Confederate Positions July 2-3, 1863

Young Captain Fassitt's part in this action is described in the 1901 history, *Deeds of Valor.* [11]

It was on the day before the demonstration known as Pickett's charge that Captain John B. Fassitt of Company F, Twenty-third Pennsylvania Infantry, displayed his courage, his quick mind, action and willingness to shoulder great responsibility.
On the day of the Peach Orchard struggle, shortly after Major-General Daniel E. Sickles had received the wound, which later cost him a leg, that Battery I, of the Fifth United States Artillery, was captured by the Confederates. Captain Fassitt, at the time was senior aide to General Birney, who, General Sickles having been carried off the field was in command of the Third Army Corps. Fassitt had just completed the work of reforming Humphrey's Division on Cemetery Ridge after it had been driven back from Blodensburg Road, and was returning to the left line to report to General Birney, when he saw Lieutenant Samuel Peoples of Battery I, standing on a rock looking to the front. Thereupon Captain Fassitt asked the lieutenant why he was not with his battery, and the lieutenant answered: "Because it has just been captured." And then pointing toward his battery, the lieutenant continued: "And if those Confederates are able to serve my guns, those troops you have just been forming on the ridge, won't stay there a minute."

Captain Fassitt, instantly comprehending the fact that the battery could direct an enfilading fire on Cemetery Ridge, and recognizing that ridge as the key to the Federal position, he rode rapidly to the nearest troops- the Thirty-ninth New York Infantry-and ordered Major Hillebrandt, the commanding officer, to retake the battery. "By whose orders?" asked the major. The captain replied: "By order of General Birney" I am in General Hancock's Corps," responded the major. To this the captain said: "Then I order you to take those guns, by order of General Hancock."

At this, Major Hillebrandt moved his regiment by flank[12] *with superb alacrity (sic), and when opposite the battery, he ordered a charge. Captain Fassitt not only helped to move the regiment by the flank, but, being the only mounted officer, also assisted in the assault. The Confederates were not willing to give up the battery and position without a struggle and the fight was a fierce one. As the Federal line reached the Confederates, one of them seized the bridle of Captain Fassitt's horse while another raised his musket fair into the face of the mounted man. The captain struck up with his sabre just in time to divert the musket ball so that it passed through the visor of his cap, and the next instant a member of the Thirty-ninth ran his bayonet through the man who delivered the shot, while Fassitt shot down the man holding the bridle of his horse. Again free, the captain went on with Major Hillebrandt's troops, until they had secured Cemetery Hill."*

GETTYSBURG: THE THIRD DAY

On the third day of the battle, Lee attempted to overwhelm the Union forces on Cemetery Hill in what became known as "Pickett's Charge" of twelve-thousand five hundred soldiers. The Union Army was so well positioned along the ridge that they devastated the Confederate infantry, half of whom never returned to their lines. Lee was forced to retreat the next day to Virginia; the battle and Lee's hope of invading the North were over.

JOHN BARCLAY FASSITT AFTER THE WAR

Following his discharge from the Army, Fassitt stayed in touch with his Civil War colleagues as an active member of the veteran's organization, the Third Army Union. He was a businessman in New York for a number of years. In the 1880s, he had government appointments as Postage Stamp Agent for the United States Post office Department at a salary of $2500 per year, and as Chief Deputy United States Marshall for the District of Columbia. In 1886 he joined the E.K. Willard banking and brokerage firm.

He did not marry until he was fifty-four years old[13]; his bride Amelia Ely Augusta was the widow of a banker. In October 1894, public records show that Major John Barclay Fassitt applied for a passport[14], indicating that he intended to travel in Europe, Asea (sic) and Africa. Two months later he received the announcement of the Medal of Honor Award. The recognition came thirteen years prior to his death in 1907.

JOHN B. FASSITT
Wearing the Medal of Honor

THE MEDAL OF HONOR

As was the case with many Civil War veterans, Fassitt's heroism was not officially recognized until decades after the event, when in preparation for a general reunion of survivors of the Third Army Corps, his comrades in arms petitioned the then-Secretary of War for the Medal of Honor. Fassitt's medal was awarded on December 29th, 1894, one of a total of sixty-four[15] related to the Gettysburg battle.

The citation reads[16]:

The President of the United States of America, in the name of Congress, takes pleasure in presenting the Medal of Honor to Captain John Barclay Fassett, United States Army, for extraordinary heroism on 2 July 1863, while serving with Company F, 23d Pennsylvania Infantry, in action at Gettysburg, Pennsylvania. While acting as an aide, Captain Fassett voluntarily led a regiment to the relief of a battery and recaptured its guns from the enemy.

The Medal is the highest military decoration awarded by the United States Government and is bestowed on a member of the United States Armed Forces whose actions are distinguished "...conspicuously by gallantry and intrepidity at the risk of his life above and beyond the call of duty while engaged in an action against an enemy of the United States..." It is commonly presented posthumously.

For the period between the Revolutionary War and the War Between the States, the American military had no formal way of rewarding individual gallantry by way of medals. Distaste for a reminder of the British uniforms decked with rows of medals evidently influenced for many years the attitude of the military brass.

Early in the Civil War conflict, the United States Navy initiated the concept of Medals of Honor to "promote the efficiency of the Navy", followed shortly thereafter by the Army. In 1862 a measure was signed into law awarding a Medal of Honor for non-commissioned officers and privates, which was amended in 1863 to include all officers. Although the award was created for the Civil War, it was made a permanent decoration by Congress also in 1863.

Debates occurred throughout until the end of the 1800s as to the eligibility for the award; the final tally for the Civil War was 1200 soldiers, 310 sailors and 17 marines. For service at Gettysburg, nineteen medals were awarded during the war and another three in the decade following. Forty-one more were awarded between 1880 and 1907, for a total of sixty-three. (A sixty-fourth Gettysburg medal was authorized as late as the year 2014 for the bravery of Lieutenant Alonzo H. Cusing.)

MORE SIGNATURES IN JOHN FASSITT'S ALBUM

The West Collegiate School class, in which the young John Fassitt found himself, produced more individuals noted for remarkable achievements later in life. They included:

Isidor Loewenthal[17], 24 year-old teacher at the school, on November 21st, 1849, placed his signature in the album, beneath two lines of Arabic text.

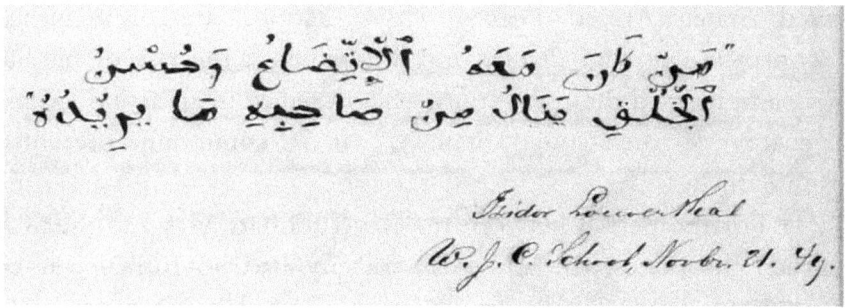

Signature of Isidor Loewenthal in John Fassitt's album 1849

Loewenthal was a Polish Jew, born in Poznan. As a result of a political poem that he published he was compelled to flee the country, and arrived in New York in the autumn of 1846. He converted to Christianity and quickly mastered the English language, acting at the same time as tutor of French, German, and Hebrew. He taught for four years at the Collegiate School in Mount Holly, New Jersey. He was ordained an evangelist in New York, and departed for India in August 1856, with the object of establishing a mission among the Afghans of the Punjab. He became fluent in Pushtu, the Afghan language, and learned to preach also in Persian, Arabic, and Hindustani. In the seven years of his missionary life at Peshawar he published a translation of the New Testament in Pushtu, and had nearly completed a dictionary of that language before his death in 1864. He was accidentally slain, in his garden at night, by an attendant, who mistook him for a robber. His grave is in the British cemetery in Peshawar.

Grave of ISODORE LOWENTHAL
Peshawa, Pakistan

Thirteen-year old George Frederick Bensell[18], of Germantown Pennsylvania, quoted Byron:

> *Between two worlds life hovers like a star*
> *'Twixt night and morn, upon the horizon's verge*
> *How little do we know that which we are*
> *How less what we may be! the eternal surge*
> *Of time and tide rolls on and bears afar*
> *Our bubbles; as the old burst new emerge,*
> *Lash'd from the foam of ages; while the graves*
> *Of empires heave but like some passing waves.*

Born in Philadelphia, Bensell studied at the Pennsylvania Academy of Fine Arts and became a painter of portraits, poetical genre subjects, landscape, and historical works. He was also an illustrator of books and magazines. The Philadelphia Sketch Club, America's first such organization for artists, was formed in his studio in 1860, and he served as the Club's first president.

ABOUT THE NAME "WEST JERSEY"[19]

For the short period between 1674 and 1704, New Jersey consisted of two separate proprietary colonies, with provincial capitals in Perth Amboy, close to New York (East Jersey) and Burlington, on the Delaware River and closer to Philadelphia (West Jersey). The boundary passed from Little Egg Harbor, located about midway along the state's Atlantic shoreline, to the Delaware Water Gap, about thirty miles south of the northernmost point in the state.

Even after the union of East and West Jersey in 1704 to form New Jersey, the government of the state was still formally split until the end of the Colonial period. It was not until after the end of the Civil War that New Jersey-ites started to use the terms of South Jersey and North Jersey, as they do today, with the centers of cultural and linguistic influence being Philadelphia and New York respectively. To this day the phrase "West Jersey" still exists in telephone listings for certain companies and institutions.

Notes:

[1] John Barclay Fassitt's Album:

        Publisher: None: blank desk notebook.
        Dimensions: 8 X 6 inches
        Covers: Marbled paper over boards, leather spine.
        Pages: Machine lined, hand numbered.
        First entry: 1850

[2] Annual Report of the Pennsylvania Railroad Company: At a meeting of the Stockholders, James Fassitt Esq. was elected chairman, Dec 6, 1847.

[3] Ancestry.com: US Census 1850: list of staff and students at the school in West Holly, NJ.

[4] Ancestry.com: U.S. Civil War soldiers records, Aaron Brainard Jerome.

[5] www.onlinebiographies.info *Biography of Mrs. Mary C. McDonald, wife of William McDonald.*

[6] From the *Harvard College Class of 1858, 30 Year Report:*

JOHN BARCLAY FASSITT — He left our class during the second term of our freshman year, and went into the wholesale dry-goods-business in Philadelphia. At the breaking out of the war, he was travelling in the South. He returned to Philadelphia, and in April 1861, went out with the Philadelphia City Troop, of which he was a member, for the three-months' campaign. At its close he was mustered out, and immediately remustered as second lieutenant, Company H, Twenty-third Pennsylvania Volunteers. During the three-months' service, he was in the battles of Falling Waters and Martinsburg with the City Troop. Was promoted first lieutenant and adjutant of his regiment, July 2, 1861. Served for a time as acting adjutant-general of brigade, but returned to his regiment just before they started for the Peninsula under General McClellan; was with it in the march up and down the Peninsula, was in the battles of Warwick Creek, Williamsburg, Seven Pines, and the seven-days' fighting around Richmond. Promoted captain on the field at Malvern Hill, for "gallant and meritorious conduct in the face of the enemy." Was in the battles of Chantilly and Fredericksburg with his regiment; then returned to General Birney's staff, and was in the battle of Gettysburg and all the fights in which the Third Corps was engaged till the Grant campaign around Richmond, when he was ordered to Washington as President, General Court Martial. Served temporarily on the staffs of Generals Stoneman and Sickles. At the close of the war came to

New York. Was appointed, Jan. I, 1883, Chief Deputy United States Marshal for the District of Columbia. Was appointed, March , 1885, Postage Stamp Agent for the United States. Jan. 1, 1886, resigned to go into business with E. K. Willard & Co., bankers and brokers, New York City.

[7] Wikipedia: Battle of Gettysburg.

[8] Gardner, Alexander. *Gardner's Photographic Sketch Book of the War:* Philip & Solomons, Washington,1865-66

[9] http://www.gdg.org/Gettysburg%20Magazine/devil.html An Analysis of the Buford manuscripts.

[10] https://commons.wikimedia.org/wiki/File:FieldOfGettysburg1863.PNG This oval-shaped map depicts Gettysburg Battlefield during July 1st, 2nd & 3rd, 1863. Prepared by Theodore Ditterline and published in Philadelphia by P. S. Duval & Son; the map reveals the troop and artillery positions and movements.

[11] Beyer, Walter F. & Keydel, Oscar F. *Deeds of Valor: How America's Heroes Won the Medal of Honor.* Published by Perrien – Keydel Co., Detroit 1902.

[12] "by flank" was a military terms for "sideways."

[13] Ancestry.com: New York Times marriage index 1890. Issue date Dec 11, 1890. Bride's father's name Hon. Nathan C. Ely.

[14] US Passport application dated Oct 17, 1894. Major John Barclay Fassitt was described as:

Stature: 5 feet 8 ½ inches	Forehead: high
Eyes: grey	Nose: straight
Mouth: medium	Chin: round
Hair: grey	Complexion: dark
Face: oval	

[15] Wikipedia: List of Medal of Honor recipients for the Battle of Gettysburg.

[16] http://valor.militarytimes.com/recipient.php?recipientid=1844 Military Times Hall of Valor, John Barclay Fassett.

[17] *Appleton's Cyclopaedia of American Biography*. Published by D. Appleton & Company, NY Volume 4, 1888.

[18] Wikipedia: George Frederick Bensell (1837 – 1879).

[19] www.westjersey.org: West Jersey and South Jersey Heritage: website devoted to the History of South Jersey and its roots in the Quaker colony of West Jersey (1674 to 1703)

CHAPTER 5
THE AGE OF CONFEDERATE INDEPENDENCE

Charles H Smith, also known as "Bill Arp."

Harriet Smith was the owner of a "Confessions Album[1]," designed to elicit a written portrait of an inscriber through questions about opinions and attitudes. She was one of twelve children of Charles H. Smith[2] a Southern humorist and devoted Confederate, who wrote under the pen name "Bill Arp." Harriet's album contains some decidedly pro-Confederacy sentiments.

THE SMITH FAMILY OF ROME GEORGIA

The famous or infamous "March to the Sea" ordered by Union General William Tecumseh Sherman[3] is described in the popular song as having been "from Atlanta to the Sea." In fact the destruction commenced in the town of Rome, Georgia, sixty-six miles northwest of Atlanta. Sherman's orders to General John Corse in Rome had called for the destruction of "… all public property not needed by your command, all foundries, mills, workshops, warehouses, railroad depots … and bridges." Five days later, when Sherman commenced his march in Atlanta on November 15th, 1864, the smoke was still rising from Rome's burned out buildings.

In the months prior to the 1864 arrival of Union troops in north Georgia, eight-year-old Harriet had moved together with the rest of her family, from Rome to perceived safety first in Atlanta, Georgia and then in Alabama. When the Smith family eventually returned they found that their home, which had been used by several Union generals including Sherman, had been sacked and gutted.

Harriett Hutchins Smith[4], or Hattie, was the fourth of the twelve children born to Charles Henry Smith, a lawyer, and Mary Octavia Hutchins, daughter of a judge who owned a Chattahoochee River plantation, which was worked by over one hundred slaves.

Shortly after her sixteenth birthday, Hattie was given the album, titled "Mental Photographs." The first written entry is from 1872, almost seven years after the end of the Civil War. Hattie, and most of the friends who wrote in her album, would have experienced the tribulations of the conflict as young children, and in the case of the Smith family the hardship of evacuation and return to a home that had been destroyed.

MENTAL PHOTOGRAPHS: AN ALBUM FOR CONFESSION OF TASTES, HABITS AND CONVICTIONS

HARRIET SMITH'S album 1872

Harriet Smith's album has thirty-eight pairs of pages for invited individuals to complete answers to forty questions. Between 1872 and 1878, the queries are answered by family members and by friends of the young woman. The writing from the 1870s is invariably in ink, and in the disciplined style that children were being taught at that time. From the years 1891 to 1902 the entries are from Harriett's four daughters, and the writing is mostly in pencil.

The entries on the two pages reproduced here were written in 1872 by a recently graduated lawyer, twenty-four-year-old Hamilton Yancey[5]. Yancey's father had served as a colonel in the Confederate forces during the Civil War.

Question: Your favorite character in history?
Answer: "Our Own Lee."

AGE OF CONFEDERATE INDEPENDENCE

Question: What epoch would you choose to have lived in?
Answer: "The Age of Confederate Independence."

Question: What is your favorite amusement?
Answer: "Hunting Doodles." (i.e. Yankee soldiers)

Question: What are the saddest words?
Answer: "It might have been."

A few of the responses from the years 1872 through 1878 were peculiar to the Southern location.

Your favorite flower:
> Magnolia was the most popular answer.

Your favorite perfume:
> The smell of violets was a popular response.

Your favorite character in history:
> The most frequent answer was Robert E. Lee; another was Jefferson Davis. In no instance was it Abraham Lincoln

What epoch would you choose to live in?
> In addition to Hamilton Yancey's "in the age of Confederate Independence", another was "from 1800 to April 1865." Most others were "In the present."

Where would you like to live?
> The answers ranged from "In the land of cotton" to "In the sunny south" to "Rome, Georgia"; other choices were "Florida" and "California."

What are the saddest words?
> One answer, in 1877, was "Ruined by cheap Chinese labor," a quote from an 1870s poem[6] by Bret Harte, intended by the poet to be a satirical commentary on racial prejudice.

BILL ARP

Harriett's father Charles Henry Smith was a much-loved Southern author writing under the pseudonym "Bill Arp." He was an ardent Confederate, and was appointed to the rank of major in the Confederate States Army. After he was invalided out in 1863, he is said to have remarked, "I joined the army and succeeded in killing about as many of them as they of me." A long-time writer for *The Atlanta Constitution* newspaper, he made a name for himself as a humorist shortly after the South left the Union when he wrote the first of the satirical letters, from a supposed simple Georgia cracker[7] named Bill Arp. He continued to write for forty-two years. Like Joel Chandler Harris and other humorists in this period, Smith wrote in the so-called "cracker" dialect of Georgia and Florida. The great popularity of his letters caused him to emerge from the war as "a Southern institution, a kind of national jester for the Confederacy."

The name Bill Arp came into being when Smith decided that the proclamation of Abraham Lincoln, issued after the surrender of Fort Sumter, calling forth states militias, was "very absurd and ridiculous." To vent his feelings at Lincoln's words, he wrote a satiric response, which he addressed to Mr. Abe Linkhorn, in the form of a supposedly friendly letter of well-meaning advice from a semi-literate backwoodsman. Among the listeners, when he read this letter from the steps of the Rome courthouse, was a man named Bill Arp. Because he agreed with the sentiments expressed in the letter, Arp asked Smith to put his name on it when it would be published. Smith continued to use the pseudonym to write about issues that he couldn't discuss as a public figure.

The wartime Bill Arp letters were published as "Bill Arp, So Called: A Side Show of the Southern Side of the War." Smith's last collection of letters, published in 1903, was titled "Bill Arp: From the Uncivil War to Date."[8] In 1887, the Smiths moved to Cartersville, Georgia. For the Smiths' 50th wedding anniversary, Joel Chandler

Harris sent a cake knife inscribed "To Bill Arp from Uncle Remus." Smith died and was buried in Cartersville in 1903. After his death, schools and parks in Georgia and even a town in Texas were named in honor of Bill Arp. His wife, Mary, passed away six years later.

HARRIET SMITH LATER

On October 20th, 1881 in Bartow County, GA Harriett Smith married[9] George Aubrey, a lawyer. They had five children, four girls and a boy. Harriett died in Cartersville in 1953 at the age of ninety-seven. Her oldest daughter Rosa was eighty-nine at her death in 1971 at Richland, South Carolina, the area from which the album was obtained.

Notes:

[1] Harriet Smith's Album:

	Publisher:	Holt & Williams, New York
	Dimensions:	8 ¼ X 7 inches
	Covers:	Green leather over boards. Gilt-stamped "MENTAL PHOTOGRAPHS IMPERIAL EDITION"
	Pages:	Title Page "MENTAL PHOTOGRAPHS, AN ALBUM FOR CONFESSIONS OF TASTES, HABITS and CONVICTIONS." Edited by Robert Saxton. Pages printed in pairs with 40 questions and spaces for entering answers.
	First entry:	1872

[2] http://www.aboutnorthgeorgia.com/ang/Charles_Henry_Smith_('Bill_Arp') *Georgia's Premier Humorist* by Carole E. Scott 2001.

[3] http://www.ourgeorgiahistory.com/ogh/march_to_the_sea "March to the Sea" a chronology of Sherman's campaign:

November 9, 1864 General William Tecumseh Sherman issued the first orders directly related to his "March to the Sea." Over the next few days the city of Rome, GA would be destroyed and track from Atlanta to Chattanooga torn up, some transported to Tennessee for later use, some twisted into "Sherman's hairpins" and left by the side of the railroad.

November 10, 1864 General John Corse ordered infrastructure in Rome, GA destroyed if it could be used for war. Among the buildings burned were two depots, warehouses, and a grist mill.

[4] Ancestry.com: Emory family Tree: Harriet Hutchins Smith.

[5] Knight, Lucian L. *A Standard History of Georgia and Georgians.* (Includes Hamilton Yancey's biography), Lewis Publishing Company, Chicago, 1917.

[6] Harte, Francis Bret. *The Heathen Chinee.* (A satire of racial prejudice in Northern California, which was, however, embraced by the American public as a mockery of Chinese immigrants, and that greatly shaped anti-Chinese sentiment at the time.)

[7] One meaning of the term "cracker" related to the extended informal discussions carried on by persons habitually assembled at a country store, hence *cracker-barrel philosophy.*

[8] Smith, Charles Henry. *Bill Arp: From the Uncivil War to Date, 1861-1903*. The Hudgins Publishing Company, Atlanta, 1903,

[9] Ancestry.com: G.H. Aubrey married H.H. Smith

CHAPTER 6
UNION OFFICER & VIGILANTE

MAUDE KING'S album 1899

The family name Vanzandt on entries in Maude King's album is the link to Maude's stepfather, Civil War soldier Captain James R. Vanzandt. He was present at two of the early battles, Wilson's Creek and Pea Ridge, that were pivotal to the fate of the State of Missouri.

Maude's mother, Mary Permelia Stallcup King, had been widowed for less than a year when she married the Civil War Union veteran. Vanzandt was also a latter-day organizer of a group of vigilantes in Taney County[1], Missouri, whose nickname "The Baldknobbers" lives on in one of the principal entertainment attractions in Branson, the Ozark vacation destination.

THE ALBUM

Page in MAUDE KING'S album 1899 with an entry
from Kirbyville, MO

Maude King's album[2] was found in an antique shop in Branson, Missouri, fewer than seven miles from Kirbyville, the village where its former owner lived and where she asked her relatives and friends to write in her book. Most of the thirty inscriptions were made in pencil on pages that are now beginning to crumble with age. Many entries gave Kirbyville as the location.

Maude was one of the five children of Samuel King[3] and his wife, Mary Permelia Stallcup. A few months after Samuel died in 1896, Mary Permelia, then forty-one years old, married recently widowed, seventy-one-years-old James Rollins Vanzandt. A year later the couple had a daughter, who they named Missouri Ann Vanzandt.

In 1899 when twenty-one-year old Maude presented her album for inscriptions, she had four siblings ranging in age from nine to twenty-five, and eleven stepsiblings with ages from three to forty-seven[4]. Maude's younger sisters, Lula, Lina and "Moe" King were among the signers. Her thirty-five-year-old stepbrother James Vanzandt and his wife Clara wrote in the album, as did her stepsisters-in-law Margaret and Maud Vanzandt, as well as Cora, the twelve-year-old step-niece who provided the verse below.

Miss Maude King   Dear Friend:

You I love and will forever
You may change but I will never
Time may roam and friends may part
But that will never change my heart
Your friend, Cora Vanzandt

Kirbyville, MO Dec. 14 1899

JAMES ROLLINS VANZANDT

To say that James Vanzandt had an interesting life would be an understatement. In the year 1915, the *White River Leader* [5] newspaper in Branson, Missouri, published a series of "Incidents, Adventures and Reminiscences as told by some of the Old Settlers of Taney County." The following is excerpted from Vanzandt's account of his life in his own words.

> *"Howdy do, howdy do; will you light and come in?" This was the greeting of Captain Vanzandt of Kirbyville to a party of visitors. The Captain, or Uncle Jimmy, as he is affectionately called by the people of Kirbyville and Taney County, is ninety years young.*
>
> *As we accepted his invitation to light, Uncle Jimmy came out and gave each some appropriate greeting. "So you're from Tennessee; you're mine then ...I was born in Tennessee, six miles east of Chattanooga, with Lookout Mountain and Missionary Ridge only five miles away.*
>
> *"Yes, I married my first wife back in Tennessee. Mother said one day, 'Jimmy, you ought to get married. I need somebody to help me with the work.' I said, 'All right, mother, just pick out the one you want: I can get any of them.' So mother picked out the girl, and I married her and brought her home. Have twelve children in the family, besides raising three grandchildren -- fifteen in all -- and never had a doctor in the*

house for any of us. It's always been my opinion if half the doctors were dead and the other half so sick they couldn't get out, there'd be more of us folks alive.

"I've cut fifteen cords of wood this fall. I don't need anyone to cut wood for me. I've always been active; that's the reason I'm so young at ninety. More people die of laziness than die of hard work. A man's got to work and exercise to live a long life.

"Oh, yes; I often walk to Branson and back; less trouble to walk than to go over to the farm and saddle a horse.

"Yes, [the present conflict in Mexico] takes me back to years ago, when I fought through the Mexican War. Started in 1848, and went all through the war. Was under General Scott, and went from Vera Cruz to Jalapa, Chapultepek [sic], Molino del Rey, and on to the City of Mexico. When we stormed the fortress of Chapultepek we went like coons up a tree, and lots of Mexicans fired their guns and then threw themselves from the cliffs and killed themselves to keep from falling into our hands. They thought we'd torture them like they did their prisoners.

"I saw Stonewall Jackson in the Mexican War, and again in the Civil War.

"Yes, I came to Missouri from Tennessee in '53 - drove three yoke of cattle, and some horses. We started the 3rd of May and reached Springfield the 10th of June. We had good luck all the way; our children were with us, and nobody was sick during the whole time.

"I went into the Union Army in 1861, in Company K, 24th Missouri Infantry. I organized the first company of Union soldiers that went out of Springfield. Lots of my friends went into the Southern army, but I said I had fought for this nation in one war, and couldn't go back on her now. After the battle of Pea Ridge, I had 800 prisoners to take to Springfield, Illinois, to the Federal Prison. We went from Cassville to Springfield, Missouri, and from there to Springfield, Illinois, and I treated those men just like I did myself.

"Near the beginning of the War, a pontoon bridge of heavy canvass (sic) boats was sent to Batesville, Arkansas, to span the White River there, and seven engineers were sent along to put it up. *They worked three weeks and didn't accomplish a thing. I happened to say to an English sergeant in my company that I could put that bridge up in a day. What I said got to the ears of General Curtis, and he ordered me to do the work. I ran off the seven engineers, and my men and I had the bridge done in two hours. Then I was ordered to take charge of the bridges.*

"We always knew when a battle was coming on, for we got only about half rations for a day or two before. Take a man when he is hungry, if you want him to fight. He goes into battle like a mad hog then. ...No, never was hurt; went all through the war without a scratch.

"What do I think of most in these later days? Well, I hold that the first impressions we get in life are with us when we die, and the first impressions are from our mothers. Mother lived with me always, and she was the head of our house as long as she lived. I never bought a new dress or pair of shoes for my wife without getting them for my mother, too."

VANZANDT: THE UNION ARMY OFFICER

When the Civil War started, James Vanzandt was thirty-six years old and a veteran of the Mexican-American War of 1846-1848, in which he participated under General Winfield Scott. Among the battles cited by Vanzandt was the taking of Chapultepec Castle[6], in September 1847; he mentioned the presence of then-Lieutenant Thomas J. "Stonewall" Jackson. In addition to Jackson, other junior officers who participated in this action and who became generals in the American Civil War fourteen years later were Ulysses Grant, and Confederates George Pickett, James Longstreet and Robert E. Lee. This battle and the achievements of the United States Marines are memorialized in the opening lines of the Marine Hymn "From the Halls of Montezuma..."

In the first months of the Civil War, it was uncertain which way the State of Missouri would go. The state's newly elected governor, Claiborne Jackson, who sympathized with the South, did not immediately advocate secession, and in February 1861, the state assembled a convention to resolve the issue, with former governor Sterling Price presiding. By the spring of 1861, the pro-secession groups under Price had taken control of the Missouri State Militia and were aligning themselves with the Confederate army. Their seizure of a small armory in the western part of the state caused the Federal Government to authorize Brigadier General Nathaniel Lyon to take the steps necessary to head off a Confederate takeover of the State of Missouri. These actions led to two military clashes, the battle of Wilson's Creek in southwest Missouri, and another at Pea Ridge, just across the state line in Arkansas. The focus was the strategically important town of Springfield, fifty miles from the Arkansas line, and sitting astride what was known as the "wire road," along the telegraph line from St. Louis to Fort Smith, Arkansas, and also the path of the Butterfield Stagecoach.

Civil war records show that James R. Vanzandt first enrolled as a First Lieutenant in the Webster County[7] Regiment Home Guard Infantry in July 1861. This unit was stationed at Springfield, Missouri until August 21, 1861, when it was disbanded in favor of a federal force. He then was commissioned an officer in the Missouri 24th Infantry[8] of the regular Union Army. He was present for the two battles, early in the War, that would determine the fate of Missouri in the war.

BATTLE OF WILSON'S CREEK, MISSOURI: JULY 1861

For the Confederates, Sterling Price and his force of more than eight thousand members of the Missouri State Guard teamed with CSA General Ben McCulloch and his forces of about twelve thousand Confederate soldiers. Price and McCulloch squabbled about who should lead the combined force. Union General Lyons Federal forces were encamped at Springfield and McCulloch's plan was to defeat them there and then move across to take St. Louis and control the entire state. In Springfield, Lyons was convinced that he must eventually retreat or be encircled by the much larger combined Confederate forces.

It was in this battle that the first general on either side was killed, General Nathaniel Lyon. Although the Confederates won the battle, they were so damaged as a fighting force that they were unable to follow up and move across Missouri; they retreated to Arkansas for the winter.

BATTLE OF PEA RIDGE, ARKANSAS: MARCH 1862

In the book *The Battle of Pea Ridge*[9], the author James Knight mentions Vanzandt's actions:

> *Major Eli Weston had been juggling his small force and defending the ground around Elkhorn Tavern as best he could for almost three hours while the enemy force grew in front of him. Soon after his troops became engaged Weston had ordered Captain J.R. Vanzandt, with his Company K, to begin moving the prisoners and the provost marshal wagons, which were parked in a field near the tavern, back to a safe area.*

In this battle two Confederate Generals were killed, McCulloch and McKintosh. After their defeat, the Confederates never again posed a serious threat to the State of Missouri.

VANZANDT: VIGILANTE

After the war, Vanzandt returned to farm in Missouri, settling in Taney County. The state had, during the conflict, been hit continuously by fighting between pro- and anti- secessionist forces. Afterwards the neighbor- versus-neighbor fighting continued throughout the state. Between 1865 and 1885, Taney County[10] reported there were 40 murders and not a single suspect was ever convicted.

In 1883, thirteen men led by former Union Army Captain Nat N. Kinney, a self-declared preacher, met to form a group to deal with the problem of lawlessness. James R. Vanzandt, by then a prominent member of the community as a farmer and also a Methodist circuit rider, was one of the leading members of this assemblage of thirteen men who called themselves both the "Citizen's Committee" and "The Law and Order League". However, because their secret meetings were held atop a "bald" mountain in order to keep a lookout for spies - the public began to refer to them as the Baldknobbers. One of their first actions was to take two men from jail and hang them.

Some of the Baldknobbers[11] adopted, as a uniform, a simple hood with corners tied off like ears, and cutout eye and mouth holes. This fearsome appearance inflamed an anti-sentiment, peaking with the formation of the anti-Baldknobbers.

Baldknobbers depicted in the 1919 Film
"The Shepherd of the Hills"

A nineteen-year-old orphan, Andy Coggburn, who led a loosely knit faction of anti-Baldknobbers, took great pleasure in deriding Kinney, pulling pranks and speaking out against the vigilante gang. Kinney and his fellow Baldknobbers held considerable pull in the county and in no time Coggburn was shot and killed by Kinney in "self-defense" outside the local church where Kinney had gone to preach that night. Vigilante outrages continued for a time until their opponents succeeded in petitioning the Missouri Governor to send an Adjutant General to investigate the situation in Taney County. The next day a formal dissolution ceremony was held in the town square where the Baldknobbers were publicly disbanded, having served their original purpose. Two years later Kinney was shot and killed by a former member of the anti-Baldknobbers.

James Vanzandt was a prominent member of the group when it formed, but his later recollections omitted any reference to the self-appointed law-enforcers, whom he had once helped to organize.

MAUDE KING

Little more is known definitively about Maude King after December 1899, the date of the last of the entries in her album. She does not appear in the census for 1900. It's interesting that her album turned up so close to where she lived.

KIRBYVILLE & BRANSON: TODAY

Kirbyville is listed as an unincorporated community in Taney County, located approximately seven miles east of Branson on State Route 76. Its few streets are named for musical instruments, Fiddle, Guitar, Harp, Mandolin, etc. The Vanzandt cemetery[12], once on the old Vanzandt farm, is now on private property; the upwards of ninety identified burials include a number of members of the Vanzandt family.

Branson is now a nationally renowned tourist attraction, with a host of live music theaters. In 1959, the Mabe family established a show featuring a mix of country music and hillbilly comedy. For a name they went with the goofy-sounding "Baldknobbers Jamboree," borrowing the name from the vigilante group of the 1880s. The

Baldknobbers show, which is still running after more than fifty years, pointed the way for the development of Branson as the entertainment center of the Ozark Mountains.

The Civil War Battlefield sites of Wilson's Creek, Missouri and Pea Ridge, Arkansas are both National Military Parks. Each has an interpretive center and drive-around trail with explanations of the details of the action.

Notes:

[1] Taney County was named for Chief Justice Roger B. Taney, writer of the decision in the infamous Dred Scott case. Wikipedia, Dred Scott v. Sandford

[2] Maude King's Album:

Publisher:	Unknown: MADE IN GERMANY
Dimensions:	5 X 8 1/4 inches
Covers:	Velour fabric over boards. Originally decorated with a metal motif "Autographs".
Pages:	Title page color floral lithograph. Remainder white, faded by age to light brown.
First entry:	1899

[3] Ancestry.com: adnilj Family tree. Lula King b 1884, sister of Maude King b 1878. Father: Samuel King 1849 – 1896, mother: Mary Permelia Stallcup 1855 – 1928.

[4] Ancestry.com: adnilj Family tree. James Rollins Vanzandt, birth Oct 1, 1824, death Mar 10, 1920 in Oliver Twp., Taney Co. Missouri. Married (1) Martha Sullins Jackson 1828-1895. Married (2) Mary Permelia Stallcup 1855 – 1928.

[5] *White River Leader* newspaper, article reprinted by the White River Historical Society, 1966.

[6] Wikipedia: "Battle of Chapultepec" September 1847.

[7] http://home.usmo.com/~momollus/MOREG/HG.htm *Missouri Volunteer Forces in the Civil War.* Webster County Regiment Home Guard Infantry. Company E, James R. Vanzandt 1st Lt.

[8] Ancestry.com: U.S. Civil War Soldier records and Profiles 1861 – 1865 about James R. Vanzandt.

    Rank at enlistment: Captain
    State served: Missouri
    Survived the War: Yes
    Service record: Commissioned an officer in Company K, Missouri 24th infantry regiment. Mustered out on Mar 16, 1864

[9] *The Battle of Pea Ridge: The Civil War Fight for the Ozarks* by James R. Knight. The History Press, 2012.

[10] White River Valley Historical Quarterly, Volume 9, Number 5, Fall 1986: "Troubles in Taney County" by Douglas Mahnkey. One of a number of accounts of "The Baldknobbers".

[11] Wikipedia: "The Shepherd of the Hills." 1915 movie.

[12] White River Valley Historical Quarterly, Volume 6, number 3, Spring 1977: Vanzandt cemetery, Kirbyville, Missouri. Names of persons buried, dates born, and dates deceased.

CHAPTER 7
THE MEMPHIS LEGION

SARAH FORSTER'S album 1837

Sarah Forster Dixon and her family lived through the turmoil of the Civil War in the City of Memphis. Her husband and his prominent business friends deemed their membership in the local militia as necessary to keep them close to home for defense of the City. They called themselves the "Memphis Legion." In fact, Memphis was taken by Union forces early in the War.

Sarah pasted into her album[1] newspaper clippings with examples of poetry dedicated to the Confederate cause and soldiers.

THE CIVIL WAR IN MEMPHIS

When the American Civil War began, neither the North not the South was well prepared militarily. Just prior to the War, the standing army of the United States was just 16,000[2] men. The opposing sides each issued an immediate call to states' militias for forces. Few of these organizations had experienced anything resembling training for combat. In many cases their activities had been limited to marching in parades and drilling on parade grounds. One such organization was the Memphis Legion.

After the State of Tennessee seceded from the Union in June 1861, the western portion of the state was a Confederate stronghold, but only for a year. In February 1862 the Union Army, supported by Union Navy gunboats pushed south along the Mississippi starting from Cairo, Illinois, with the goal of controlling the entire waterway to the Gulf of Mexico, and thereby cutting off the Confederate states east of the river from those to the west.

On June 6th, 1862, in one of the shortest battles[3] of the Civil War, Union sailors took just ninety minutes to sink or capture seven of the eight boats positioned by the Confederates to protect the city. The city's mayor surrendered and Memphis was controlled by the Union for the duration of the War.

THE GREAT NAVAL BATTLE BEFORE MEMPHIS
(Wikimedia Commons)

THE MEMPHIS LEGION

The "Memphis Legion" militia, commanded by Sarah's husband Colonel L.V. Dixon, consisted primarily of wealthy city businessmen. In a volume of selected contemporary accounts of Tennessee in the Civil War[4], the compiler, under the heading "Prominent Memphis capitalists seek immunity from Confederate draft", included the following letter from the body's officers offering their services to CSA Major General Leonidas Polk, military commander of the area between the Mississippi and Tennessee Rivers.

> *MEMPHIS TENN... August 6. 1861.*
> *General L POLK, Commanding:*
> *Sir: The undersigned, officers of the Memphis Legion, beg leave to represent that since the war proclamation of President Lincoln in April last, nearly **4,000** citizens of Memphis and vicinity have gone into the Army of the Southern Confederacy, leaving at home only the heads of families and business men, who cannot go into regular service until compelled by dire necessity. Of this class about **700** have formed a military organization, known as the Memphis Legion, many members of which are of prominence and influence, who have large amounts invested in the commercial and manufacturing interests of this place and cannot leave without great pecuniary sacrifice, and, as we believe, without great inconvenience to the public. We think it to be essentially necessary that the great commercial and manufacturing interests of Memphis should be encouraged and sustained to the utmost extent, that we may continue to furnish that portion of the surrounding country with the supplies and means which are expected of us, to maintain the various relations existing between this and other communities.*
>
> *Hence, it is, we think, important that as many of our enterprising merchants and manufacturers should remain at home and so arrange their military connections as to enable them to give a considerable portion of their time to business operations. As originally intended, our organization*

contemplated no other object than the protection of our families and our homes. It is thought, however, that we can make our legion more effective for this purpose and more useful to the public by placing ourselves under your command, which we will cheerfully do provided that the War Department will receive us on the terms proposed or suggested in your memorandum to Colonel Worsham, namely, to be subject to the order of the commanding general at this place, and to be detailed for duty mainly for the defense of Memphis and immediate vicinity (with the understanding that when not on duty our members may be allowed the privilege of attending to their ordinary business).

We are led to believe that there are duties required here which can be performed by us under this arrangement. The subject of pay and subsistence, together with those of uniforms and arms, we leave to be settled by yourself and the Department, but would remark that we are poorly armed and equipped; in fact have not enough, nor but few of the right sort. We hope that you are in possession of facts enough to appreciate our motives, and will only add that if you approve of these suggestions and they are practical and proper, we will feel grateful if you will ascertain the views of the War Department on the subject, the same to be agreed upon for the term of one year.
Respectfully, your obedient servants,

L. V. DIXON Colonel

Colonel Dixon was joined by ten other officers in signing the letter.

On March 12, 1862, the Third Tennessee Infantry Battalion[5], comprised mainly of men from the Memphis Legion, was mustered into service at Memphis; its unofficial title was the "Memphis Battalion". Three months later Memphis had surrendered; the Archives of the Confederate States Army have no records of the unit actually participating in military service. Colonel Dixon and his business friends were safe.

THE DIXON FAMILY

Leonidas Virginus Dixon[6] was born at Abingdon, in southwest Virginia, into a family with strong military traditions. His grandfather, Colonel John Dixon, commanded a regiment in the American Revolutionary War. Leonidas's father, Henry St. John Dixon (1773-1846), was a fellow law student of the politician Henry Clay, graduating in 1797. He and Clay at one time talked about settling in Abingdon, Virginia. However, while Dixon stayed in Virginia to practice law, Henry Clay moved on to Kentucky and to a political career. Captain Henry Dixon served as an officer in the War of 1812. Leonidas, like his father, became a lawyer, but he chose to practice first in Mississippi and later in Tennessee.

At Vicksburg, Mississippi, in 1841 Leonidas married Sarah Jane Forster, the original owner of the album. The couple had eight children, six of whom survived into adulthood.

THE ALBUM

The first page of the leather-covered album was signed in 1839 by its original owner Miss S.J. Forster, of Jackson, Mississippi.

An additional inscription on the first page of the album from Sarah is to sixteen-year-old Leila[7], the oldest of her daughters who was then living at home. The message was on the occasion, just after the Civil War, of the mother passing the book to her daughter.

To Leila Scott Dixon,

Memphis on June 7th, 1865.

From her Mother

Title and dedication page in SARAH FORSTER'S album 1839

Some early poetical entries appear to date from the eighteen-thirties and forties. They include a full page with a poem "Hurrah to the Clay" pasted in, a tribute to Henry Clay, the law-school friend of Sarah's father in law.

Attached by pins to one page are examples of foliage, a custom for album decoration in vogue in the early nineteenth century

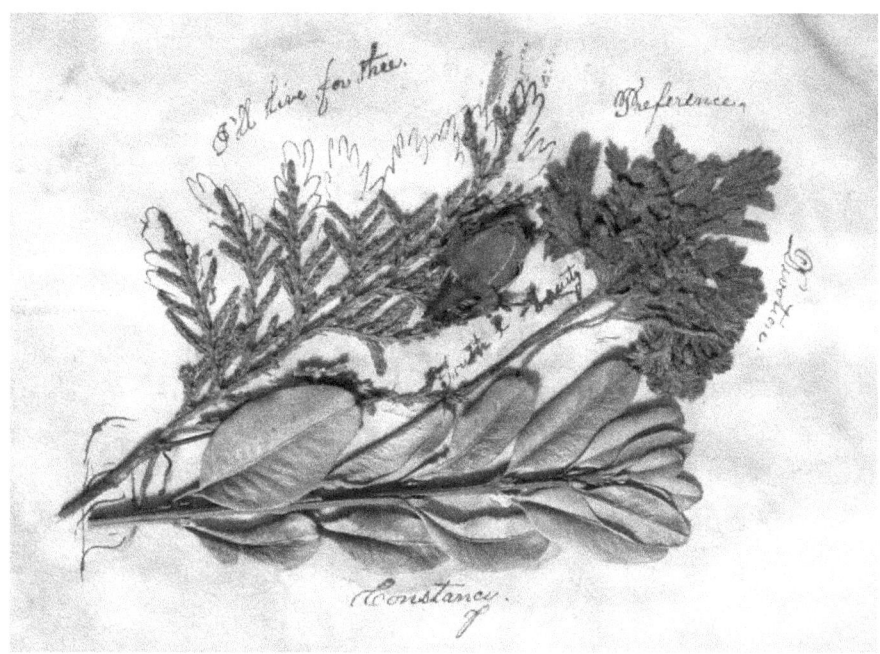

Page from SARAH FORSTER'S album with a selection of foliage with meanings attributed to the various plants.

I'll live for thee:
Preference:
Devotion:
Truth & Beauty:
Constancy.

NEWSPAPER CLIPPINGS

Sarah and her daughter evidently used the book mostly for collecting cuttings with poetry taken from newspapers and magazines. The significant bulk and inferior quality of the newsprint contributed to the poor condition of the pages and binding of the album.

Several of these inserts include poetry with post-war patriotic sentiments. In two separate clippings she selected verses from the same poem by Rev. Abram Joseph Ryan[8], sometimes known as the Poet-Priest of the South.

LINES
WRITTEN FOR THE MEMORIAL ASSOCIATON OF FREDERICKSBURG, VIRGINIA.

Gather the sacred dust
  Of the warriors tried and true,
Who bore the Flag of our Nation's trust,
And fell in the cause, though Lost, still Just,
  And died for me and you.

Gather them each and all!
  From the Private to the Chief
Come they from hovel or princely hall,
They fell for us, and for them should fall
  The tears of a Nation's grief.

The foeman need not frown:
  They are all powerless now—
We gather them here, and we lay them down,
And tears and prayers are the only crown
  We bring to wreath each brow.

And the dead thus meet the dead,
  While the living o'er them weep;
And the men whom Lee and Stonewall led,
And the hearts that once together bled,
  Together still shall sleep.

KNOXVILLE, December, 1865.

Clippings pasted into SARAH FORSTER DIXON"S album.
Verses one, two, seven and nine of the poem "Lines"
by Abram Joseph Ryan

THOUGHTS,

SUGGESTED BY THE BURIAL OF MAJOR PHIL. T. ALLIN.

Softly tread here, stranger footsteps,
  O'er the sward that bounds this grave;
Gently guard this fresh-earth hillock,
  'Neath it rests the good and brave.
Muffled footsteps sadly bore him;
  Manly comrades, with a tear,
Lightly pressed the earth around him,
  A good, brave heart lieth here.

In the home now dark and lonely,
  Hangs a sword with ivy wreathed;
Never falchion gleamed more brightly—
  Never blade more purely sheathed.
In the crimson tide of battle,
  Where the deadly breach was made
'Midst the iron thunder's rattle,
  Flashed aloft that gallant blade.

It were meet that he should rest here,
  Where the early spring flowers bloom,
Shedding pure and holy fragrance
  On the air about this tomb.
Not more blue the sky above him,
  Than his heart was brave and true;
Not more pure the orange blossoms
  Which upon his grave we strew.

In that home now draped in sorrow,
  Bending o'er the "Cloth of Gray,"
Silent, weeps one, linking with it
  Memories of her bridal day.
Holy Father! by Thy power
  Safely keep our soldier's love—
Gently bear her o'er life's journey;
  Fold her to Thyself above!

      A CONFEDERATE SOLDIER.
February 25, 1870.

Newspaper clipping of a poem citing the death of Major Phil T. Allin of Memphis.

Major Allin served under General Nathan Forrest. He died in Memphis in 1869. In 1872 a Mississippi sternwheeler steamboat the PHIL ALLIN was named after him.

THE ALBUM AFTER 1865

Additions to the album, made after the year 1865, when Sarah presented the book in 1865 to her daughter, were presumably placed by Leila Scott Dixon. In 1869, Leila noted that two examples of paper cutwork were made by her great-grandmother forty-five years earlier, in 1824.

Cutwork in the album later owned by Leila Scott Dixon

In 1873, Leila married Henry Berry, a grocer. They named their daughter, born in 1875, "Leila" after her mother. A year later the young mother died. On February 10th, 1876 the *Daily Memphis Avalanche*[9] carried this notice of the death of Leila Scott Berry:

> **BERRY** – At the residence of her husband Henry Berry, 394 Vance street, Memphis, Tennessee, on Wednesday February 8, 1876, at 6:30 p.m. Leila Scott Berry, daughter of L.V. and Sarah J. Dixon. The funeral will take place from St. Mary's Episcopal Church, Poplar Street. Services begin at 10:30 a.m. on Friday, 11th inst, and conclude in Elmwood cemetery.

A newspaper clipping pinned to the last page of the album, contains a heart-felt tribute from Leila's husband, referring to their two-year-old little girl and her dead mother.

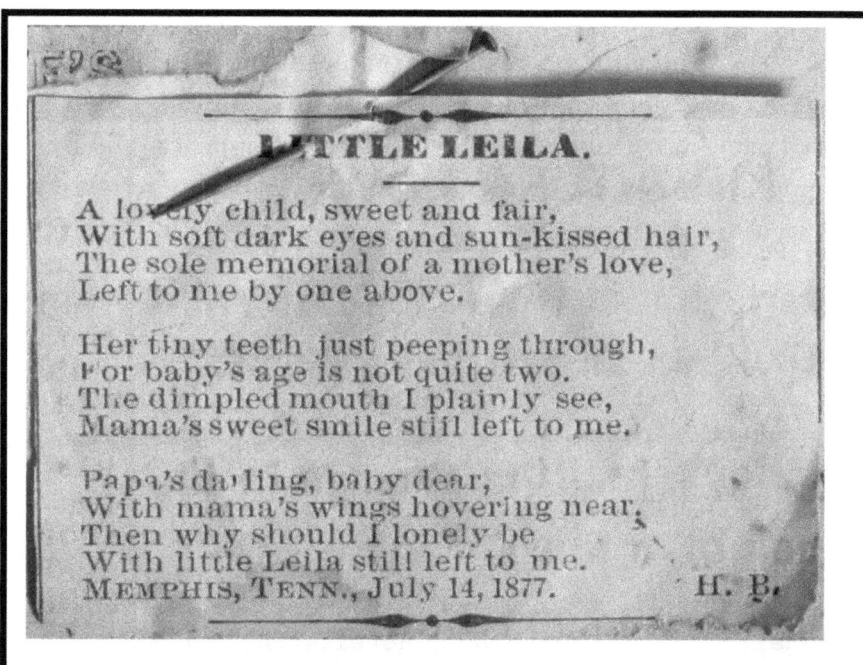

Memorial poem pinned to a page in the album of Sarah Dixon and her daughter Leila

THE YELLOW FEVER OUTBREAK OF 1878

In the summer of 1878, Yellow Fever afflicted the Mississippi River Valley from St. Louis south. In a span of five days, more than half the population of Memphis, 25,000 people, attempted to get away from the scourge by boat and by train. By October 28th, when a killing frost occurred, over 20,000 deaths had been caused. Among those who sought refuge away from the city were the Dixon family, who traveled by train to Leonidas's hometown in Virginia.

A history of the epidemic of 1878[10] includes an alphabetical list of cities and towns where the fever raged, starting with this entry:

> *ABINGDON:*
> *County seat of Washington County, Va. On the Virginia & Tennessee railroad, 189 miles from Lynchburg. Population 2100. First and only case was Judge L.V. Dixon, a refugee from Memphis, who died September 17th.*

The view at the time was that outbreaks of Yellow Fever were associated with poor sanitation.[11] News of the outbreak of epidemic created panic in neighboring states. The local newspaper, The Bristol (Virginia) News on September 24, 1878 in trying to reassure the citizens carried this story:

> The death of Judge L.V. Dixon of Memphis, at the Colonade Hotel last Tuesday has been the cause of some very unfounded alarm. Even if Judge Dixon did die of yellow fever (and this is disputed by competent authority) there would not be the slightest danger that any one else could take it there. Abingdon is nearly 2,100 feet above sea level and the disease cannot exist there. As proof of our sincerity the Editor of The News expects to go to the Abingdon Fair and to be, as usual, at the Colonade Hotel. The disease is unquestionably at Chattanooga, where some 12 deaths have occurred from it, but that city is

only 575 feet above sea level and is horribly located anyway. Abingdon is over 1400 feet higher, and the people of Abingdon might sleep with a yellow fever patient without danger.

The newspaper included this assertion from a prominent local physician:

The following from Dr. Barr is sufficient: Abingdon Va. Sept 23, 1878. My dear Sir. As it is reported that there are cases of yellow Fever in this place, I want to correct the rumor. There is no yellow fever in Abingdon. It could not exist here. Yours truly, W. Barr.

The family of the unfortunate Judge Dixon might have begged to differ.

In Elmwood Cemetery, Memphis, two years after his daughter Leila was buried, Leonidas Virginias Dixon[12] was laid to rest. Sarah Jane Forster Dixon was buried beside him in 1890.

Notes:

[1] Sarah Forster Dixon's Album:

Publisher:	J.C. Riker, New York
Dimensions:	7¾ X 6 inches
Covers:	Black embossed leather over boards. Gilt-stamped "ALBUM" on spine.
Pages:	Title page "ALBUM". Published by J.C. Riker, 15 Ann Street, New York 1835. White pages, some with black & white engravings.
First entry:	1839

[2] Wikipedia: Militia (United States) Civil War "Just prior to the War, the total peace-time army consisted of a paltry 16,000 men".

[3] Wikipedia: First Battle of Memphis

[4] Jones, James B. (compiler).*Tennessee in the Civil War: Selected Contemporary Accounts of military and Other Events.* Published by McFarland, 2011

[5] Familysearch.org: 3rd Battalion, Tennessee Infantry (Memphis Battalion),

[6] Ancestry.com: Kuehter family tree: Leonida Virginus Dixon birth Jun 30, 1816 in Washington County, VA

[7] Ancestry.com: United States 1870 Census. Leila Dixon was 18 years old, daughter of L.V. Dixon 54 and Sarah J. Dixon 48.

[8] The Rev. Abram Joseph Ryan (1838 – 1886) was an active proponent of the Confederates States of America and poet celebrated as the "Poet Laureate of the Confederacy."

[9] *Daily Memphis Avalanche*: Interment in Elmwood Cemetery, Memphis, Feb 10, 1876, Leila Scott berry daughter of L.V. and Sarah J. Dixon.

[10] Murtough, Peter. *Condensed history of the Great Yellow Fever Epidemic of 1878*. (List of Cities and Towns where the fever raged.) Toof Publishing, Memphis, 1879.

[11] Wikipedia: Memphis, Until the year 1880 when an artesian well were created, Memphis had no waterworks comparable to most large cities in America at the time; the city relied upon the river and on rainwater cisterns for its water supply. Additionally, the city had no sewage removal system. The combination of a rapidly growing population and unsanitary conditions put the citizens in harm's way for a serious epidemic, and the outbreak of yellow Fever in 1878 was so attributed. Later in the nineteen century it was established that the disease was spread by the mosquito vector *Aedes aegypti*.

[12] www.findagrave.com: Judge Leonidas Virginius Dixon, death Sep 17, 1878. Abingdon, Washington County, VA., burial Elmwood Cemetery.

CHAPTER 8
VERSES FOR SONS AND BROTHERS

LYDIA RISE'S album 1858

As one after another of her three brothers enlisted in the Union Army, Lydia Rise's autograph album[1] became a repository for patriotic poetry cut from pages of a Pennsylvania newspaper.

In addition to the hopes and fears of the family of the soldiers, the verses talked to the War's events, Northern heroes and Confederate foes.

THE RISE FAMILY

Lydia's father, Samuel Rise, died in 1850[2], leaving his widow Juliana to run the family's hotel in Lebanon, Pennsylvania, and to raise the children. Just a year before the Civil War started, the 1860 United States Census[3] tabulated the Rise family:

Juliana Rise, age 37, widow, hotelkeeper, real estate value $6,000. Juliana's children were listed as: Henry age 17, machinist apprentice; George age 13; Lydia age 14; Adam age 13.

THREE BROTHERS GO TO WAR

At seventeen years of age, Henry Rise was the first of the brothers to join the Union Army. When he enlisted in the Pennsylvania 5th Infantry[4] on April 20th, 1861, less than a week had passed since President Abraham Lincoln, following the bombardment and surrender of Fort Sumter, called for "the militia of the several States of the Union, to the aggregate number of 75,000" to serve for 90 days to suppress the rebellion. At the end of his three-month term Henry was mustered out, only to re-enlist in October, soon after his eighteenth birthday, as a sergeant in the Pennsylvania 93rd Volunteer Infantry.

Harry, as he preferred to be called, was wounded three times in action. The first time, in May 1862, was during the regiment's first battle at Williamsburg, Virginia. Less than a month later, when the regiment suffered heavy losses at the battle of Fair Oaks, Virginia, he was wounded a second time.

The official history of Pennsylvania Volunteer Infantry[5] regiments has this to say about his third injury, sustained in May 1863, during the Battle of Salem Heights, at Rappahannock River, Virginia.

Sergeant Harry G. Rise, of Company K, in a letter to his mother at home, wrote:

I had a race with the 'Rebs'; they tried to capture me. The foremost 'Reb' was shot by a friend of mine, when we both made our escape.'
Sergeant Rise was first shot by a Rebel, when he drew his rifle and shot him dead. After receiving the bullet wound the rebel leapt into the air and the last words uttered by Lt. Washington Brua, of Co. A., who was by the side of Sergeant Rise, and who was killed immediately afterwards were, "You are a good shot, Harry." Sergt. Rise did not desire to inform his mother that he had fired the shot at the time, and so wrote that a friend had fired the shot.

Sgt. Rise's accomplishments were acknowledged with three promotions. In November 1862 he was promoted to full First Sergeant. In April 1864 he was commissioned a second lieutenant and in January 1865 he was made full first lieutenant. At the War's ending in 1865, he mustered out at Washington, D.C.

Henry's two younger brothers also joined Pennsylvania Volunteer Infantry regiments. George enlisted in August 1862, three months before his eighteenth birthday. When Adam enlisted for a first time in July 1863, he was barely sixteen years old; the same age as many a regimental drummer boy. The next year, still short of his eighteenth birthday, Adam enlisted again as a Union soldier. All three brothers survived the War; however, Henry's experience as a soldier seems to have been the most remarkable.

LYDIA RISE'S ALBUM

Julianna presented the album to her daughter when Lydia was thirteen years old. The book, one of the larger and more elaborate available at the time, has fewer than a dozen written entries. Most noteworthy are the more than thirty newspaper clippings pressed in its pages, most containing northern patriotic Civil War poetry.

These words, from the poem "The Northern Mother" must have resonated with the mother and sister of the three Rise boys:

THE NORTHERN MOTHER

They are all in the army,
My three brave gallant boys;
They've changed the peace of home life
* For martial pomp and joys.*
It tore my heart-strings sadly
* To see them march away.*
But when their county called them
* I would not say them nay."*

There's one that grasps a true sword,
* Commissioned to command;*
There's one within the ranks found,
* With musket in his hand:*
There's one and he my youngest,
* Whose stirring drum doth beat*
The faultless, martial measure
* For proudly stepping feet.*

The list of slain and wounded
* I'll read with trembling breath,*
To see how many darling sons
* Have met untimely death.*
And should mine be among them
* And fell they there like braves,*
I would not wish them holier death,
* Nor ask them prouder graves.*

Washington, July 15, 1861   W.W.CURTIS

LAYS OF THE PEOPLE.

THE NORTHERN MOTHER.

They are all in the army,
  My three brave, gallant boys;
They've changed the peace of home life
  For martial pomp and joys.
It tore my heart-strings sadly
  To see them march away.
But when their country called them,
  I could not say them nay.

There's one that grasps a true sword,
  Commissioned to command;
There's one within the ranks found
  With musket in his hand;
There's one, and he my youngest,
  Whose stirring drum doth beat
The faultless, martial measure
  For proudly-stepping feet.

Their father fought before them
  On many a bloody plain—
At Erie and at Chippewa,
  At York and Lundy's Lane.
O, may his spirit nerve them
  When in the battle's brunt;
For should they fall, I'll know then
  They bear their wounds in front.

God shield my three brave darlings
  Throughout these crimson wars!
God help them in defending
  Our good old Stripes and Stars!
God speed them on their mission
  To quell the Rebel foe!
With strength, that each arch-traitor
  May need no second blow.

And when my youngest boy beats
  The loud long roll at night,
That tells of foes advancing,
  And bids them arm for fight,
God give unto my other boys,
  Amid the battle's flame,
To one—a dashing soul to lead,
  To one—unerring aim.

The list of slain and wounded
  I'll read with trembling breath,
To see how many darling sons
  Have met untimely death.
And should mine be among them,
  And fell they there like braves,
I would not wish them holier death,
  Nor ask them prouder graves!

Washington, July 15, 1861.   W. W. CURTIS.

Newspaper clipping of "THE NORTHERN MOTHER" pasted in LYDIA RISE'S album

ILLUSTRATED WITH THE NATIONAL FLAG

Two of the poetic-clippings were illustrated with the stars and stripes. **SCOTT AND THE VETERAN** by the American poet Bayard Taylor celebrated General Winfield Scott, hero of the War of 1812, and for twenty years from 1841 General-in-Chief of the Army. The flag is hand-colored. **OUR NATIONAL ENSIGN** was said to have been written under the influence of a Spiritualist medium, fourteen-year-old girl, Mary Jane Cunningham[6].

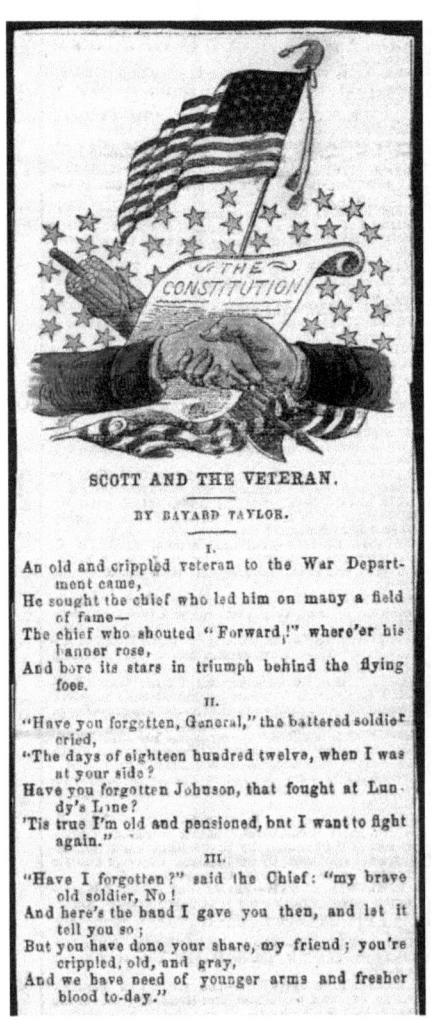

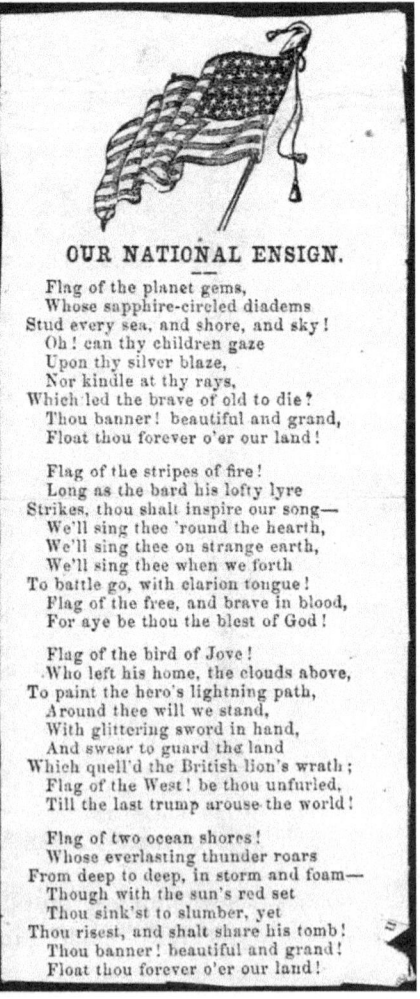

APOCALYPSE

Lydia selected the poem "Apocalypse" for her album, about a young man who, like Lydia's brother Henry, enlisted for the Union cause at the first opportunity, and at the same age:

Luther C. Ladd[7] is believed to have been the first man killed in the Civil War. He was seventeen years old at the time of his death. Luther answered President Lincoln's first call for volunteers by enlisting for three months in Company D, 6th Regt., Massachusetts Volunteers. On April 19, 1861 while marching through the city of Baltimore, this regiment was attacked by an angry secessionist mob. Luther C. Ladd was the first to fall. His injuries included a fractured skull and a fatal bullet wound.

> *Thus like a king, erect in pride,*
> *Raising his hands to heaven he cried,*
> *'All hail to the Stars and Stripes', and died.*

TWO UNION TENNESSEE HEROES

Lydia selected two poems about the loyalty to the Union of soldiers from the southern state of Tennessee. The first, The Drummer Boy of Tennessee, is described as a prose story of real life put to rhyme by a young lady. The story-poem, by Minnie Hart, about Eddie Lee the drummer boy was one of the most beloved of the War, celebrating the bravery and sacrifice of regimental boy soldiers.

> *Each soldier loved and sought to share*
> *Their part of good with him;*
> *The fifer on his back did bear*
> *Across each swollen stream*
> *This "Drummer boy" from Tennessee,*
> *Who beat with him the reveille.*

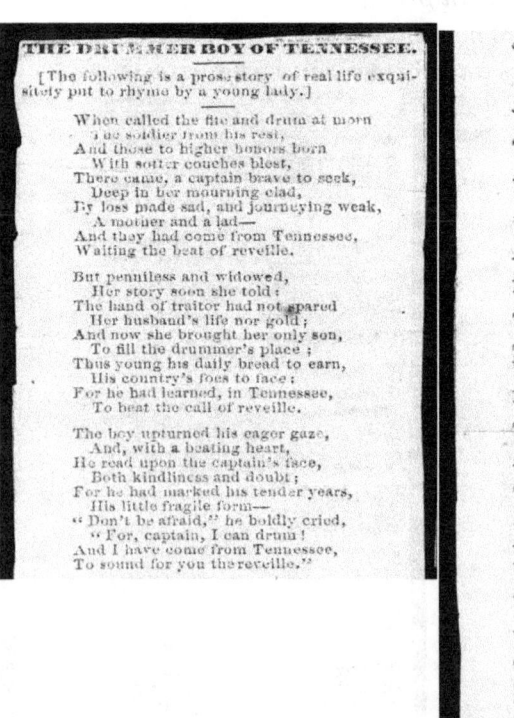

The second poem tells the story of Andrew Johnson, of Tennessee, the only senator from a seceding state to remain loyal to the Union, who risked his life to get to Washington.

The introduction to the poem reads:

Andrew Johnson, the man around whom the Unionists of East Tennessee rally has come to Washington in order that he may attend the extra session of Congress. He came by way of Cumberland Gap, where fifteen armed ruffians attempted to take his life

He says his people are willing, if need be, to die by the flag of their country on the field of battle.

Andrew Johnson, of Tennessee.

The following lines were suggested by the subjoined newspaper paragraph:

"Andrew Johnson, the man around whom the Unionists of East Tennessee rally, has come to Washington in order that he may attend the extra session of Congress. He came by way of Cumberland Gap, where fifteen armed ruffians attempted to take his life. * * * * He says that his people are willing, if need be, to die by the flag of their country on the field of battle."

His people throng around him; pl ce their safety in his hands,
For they know that he will rescue their terror-stricken land
From the grasp of armed traitors, who, by means of open fraud,
Gained their ill employed power, fearing neither man nor God!

His former friends against him! The blood-hound of the South
Upon his track! Athirst for blood, with hot and parched mouth,
They wait to slay him as he stands; but loyal, firm, and true,
He stands with mien undaunted—he'll die or fight it through!

Defend him, God of Liberty! Let not foul Treason wrest
The patriotic heart that throbs within his manly breast!
Defend him, God! A villain's act might plunge his cause in night,
And dim the hopes of thousands now gathering for the fight.

As dauntlessly he'll fling the starry flag upon the breeze,
How, in many a traitor's veins, the craven blood will freeze!
For the brave and loyal hearted shall prove that they are free,
And Anarchy be crushed in the State of Tennessee!

Then rally, rally round him! Stand up bravely for the right!
The people's will is stronger than the dread oppressor's might!
Our country's flag! unfurl it! Send forth the thrilling shout
Of thousands upon thousands! Put traitors to the rout!

So pure a cause shou'd summon ev'ry brave and upright man,
Without regard to Party, to do whate'er he can
To aid the insulted people, whom traitors seek to wrong,
And show that Truth and Justice make a Freeman's right arm strong!   W. J G
ALLENTOWN, Pa., Aug 1, 1861.

CONFEDERATE FIGURES

Some of the clippings taunted Confederate figures. The poem **JEFF. DAVIS** was written for the Rise family's local newspaper, the *Lebanon Courier*, by a student at the Swatara Institute, a private boarding school in Lebanon County. The poem opens with:

> *Jeff Davis! Jeff Davis! A traitor you are*
> *Most worthy a coating of feathers and tar!*

For the Lebanon Courier.
JEFF. DAVIS.

Jeff. Davis! Jeff. Davis! a traitor you are.
Most worthy a coating of feathers and tar!
This once peaceful country you've riven and torn.
And made all its true-hearted patriots mourn.

Jeff. Davis! Jeff. Davis! I've no doubt you think
That soon in the "White House" you'll take a big drink
Of strong whisky toddy, and shout "Here's a health
To all like myself who by stealing gain wealth."

Jeff. Davis! Jeff. Davis! you'll find that the gains
In the end, won't be worth all your trouble and pains.
Your cause you will lose, and as for the rest,
You'll find that your head's in a big hornet's nest.

Jeff. Davis! Jeff. Davis! your cake is all dough,
And one thing I'll tell you, you swimming may go.
Without any fear, as *savants* have found,
"*He that's born to be hanged will never be drowned.*"

Jeff. Davis! Jeff. Davis! though smart you may be
You "can't keep a tavern," or split up a tree
Into rails near as fast as "Old Abe," who is used
To *mauling*, you know, and his maul may be used.

Jeff. Davis! Jeff. Davis! take Saxe's advice,
And, ere rushing headlong into danger, *think twice*.
"Whenever you go to balls," battles "and that,
Look out for your head, and take care of your hat.
Else you'll find that a favorite son of your mother
Has a "brick in the one and a *ball* in the other."

HARRY C. S.

Swatara Coll. Institute, May 5th, 1861.

REBEL GENERALS

A detailed list cites Confederate Generals who had been "killed, wounded, captured, disgraced or whipped". This clipping is dated by a news item on the back referring to the Fort Wright[8] bombardment, which occurred in April 1862.

> REBEL GENERALS.—Never, we apprehend, in the annals of warfare, was a body of general officers so calamitous. Scarcely an important engagement in the whole war in which some one of them has not been either killed, wounded, captured, disgraced or whipped. The list is long and instructive:
> Robert S. Garnett, killed at Laurel Hill.
> Bernard E. Bee, killed at Bull Run.
> Francis S. Bartow, killed at Bull Run.
> Felix K. Zollicoffer, killed at Logan's Field.
> Ben M'Culloch, killed at Pea Ridge.
> James M'Intosh, killed at Pea Ridge.
> Albert S. Johnson, killed at Pittsburg.
> Phillip St. George Cooke, killed by suicide.
> Edmund K. Smith, wounded at Bull Run.
> Thomas C. Hindman, wounded at Pittsburg.
> B F. Cheatham, wounded at Pittsburg.
> Sterling Price, wounded at Pea Ridge.
> Bushrod R. Johnson, wounded at Pittsburg.
> Loyal Tilghman, captured at Fort Henry.
> Simon Bolivar Buckner, captured at Fort Donelson.
> W. M. Makall, captured at Island No. 10.
> J. N. Walker, captured at Island No. 10.
> P. Sebaum, captured at Island No. 10.
> John B. Floyd, disgraced at Fort Donelson.
> Gideon J. Pillow, disgraced at Fort Donelson.
> George B Crittenden, disgraced at Mill Spring.
> William H. Carroll, disgraced at Mill Spring.
> Henry A. Wise, disgraced everywhere.
> Richard Drayton, whipped at Port Royal.
> S. R. Anderson, whipped at Cheat Mountain.
> Humphrey Marshall, whipped at Pound Gap.
> Braxton Bragg, whipped at Pensacola and Pittsburg.
> Earl Van Dorn, whipped at Pea Ridge.
> Lawrence O'B. Branch, whipped at Newbern.
> James Jackson, whipped at Winchester.
> P. G. T. Beauregard, whipped at Pittsburg.
> William J. Hardeee, ran from Bowling Green.
> Leonidas Polk, ran from Columbus.
> Joseph E. Johnston, ran from Manassas.
> Gustavos W. Smith, ran from Manassas.
> Was there ever such a melancholy list of unfortunates? Of them no less than twenty were educated at West Point, at the expense of the Government. At least six have been members of Congress, and others in various ways honored by the Government they have made such disastrous efforts to destroy. They have served their own evil passions, and truly they have had a hard master.

RECAPTURE OF THE PRIZE SLOOP *S.J. WARING*

That the paper clippings were pressed between pages of the album, rather than pasted in, preserved access to the reverse sides of some items. In some instances, lines of news and/or advertisements revealed the dates of the newspapers. On the back of one poem was part of an article about a Civil War Maritime incident:

> RECAPTURE OF THE PRIZE SLOOP S. J. WARING.—The New York *Times* gives the following particulars of the capture and recapture of the sloop S. J. Waring, which arrived at that port on Sunday:
>
> On the third day out from New York, the 7th inst., when 150 miles from Sandy Hook, in lat. 38 degrees, long. 60 degrees, was brought to by the privateer brig Jeff. Davis, which sent a boat full of men alongside, and ordered the Captain of the schooner to haul down the United States flag, and declared her a prize to the C. S. A. They ransacked the vessel and took from her what they wanted—such as charts, quadrant, provisions, crockery, &c., and after returning to the schooner a second time they put a prize crew of five men on board without arms, and took away Captain Francis Smith, the two mates and two seamen, leaving the steward, two seamen and Mr. Bryce Mackinnon, a passenger, on board. The prize crew were Montague O'Neil, a Charleston pilot, in command; one named Stevens, as mate, and Malcolm Liddy as second mate, and two men.
>
> At 3 P. M. the schooner was headed south—probably for Charleston or near by. The remaining crew and the passengers were in hopes of a recapture by some United States vessel, and made themselves agreeable and sociable to the privateersmen, and in consequence they suspected nothing until the night of the 16th of July, when 50 miles to the southward of Charleston. Seeing no prospect of their hopes being realized, and the prize captain and first mate being asleep, the preconcerted plan was carried into effect by the steward, William Tillman, (colored,) killing the three with a hatchet, and throwing the bodies overboard. It was all finished in five minutes. One of the

The final part of the story of this episode, including the navigation back to New York, is missing from the newspaper clipping. The incident was widely reported in the press and William Tilghman was treated as a hero and was given a reward by the federal Government of six thousand dollars. The recapture of the *S.J.WARING* is the subject of a book published in 2016 *The Rest I Will Kill,* by Brian McGinty.[9]

Photo # NH 58895   Schooner S.J. Waring, recaptured from a Confederate prize crew

"S. J. WARING," RECAPTURED FROM THE PIRATES BY THE NEGRO WM. TILLMAN.

(United States Naval History Center)

THE RISE FAMILY AFTER THE WAR

Adam Good Rise was married soon after the War. The census for 1870[10] lists him as a (railroad) brakeman. He died in 1874, leaving a widow and three children.

Lydia and some of her friends traveled to San Francisco in 1866 seeking a more exciting life and more opportunities. They attended dances at the Presidio, where Lydia met her future husband, U.S. Army officer Michael J. Fitzgerald. The couple lived initially at Fort Bidwell in Modoc County, California and moved when Michael was posted to Wyoming Territory. Lydia died in 1876 in Nebraska [11] at the early age of 30.

Juliana Rise, the mother of three sons and a daughter, died in 1885 at Lebanon, PA.

George Dallas Rise seems to have been the most successful of the three brothers. In 1893 he was described in the "Proceedings of the Pennsylvania German Society"[12] as:

> *Son of Samuel Rise ... whose ancestor came to America about the year 1750 from Berne, Switzerland. He has followed printing, telegraph operating, and is now secretary of the Cornwall and Lebanon Railroad Company, treasurer of the Edison Electric illuminating Company of Lebanon, PA, Treasurer of the Lebanon and Myerstown Street railway Company and engaged in banking.*

George died in 1901 at the age of 56.

At about the same time that his sister moved to the West coast, Henry Rise also went to San Francisco, where he married a young widow from New Zealand. He was employed as a Post Office clerk[13] until sometime after 1882 when, separated from his wife, he returned to his hometown of Lebanon, where managed a livery stable for several years. Civil War hero Henry "Harry" Rise died in 1917.

RAILWAY SIGNALS

One of the clippings in the album dates from about 1887, ten years after Lydia's death. It lists the railway signals that were in use on American railroads during the latter part of the nineteenth century. How this item came to be placed in the album is not clear. In the 1890s, Lydia's brother George Rise was an officer of the Cornwall and Lebanon railroad Company. The album may have been passed down through his family.

Or, when Lydia left home to go to San Francisco, she perhaps left the book with her mother, Juliana.

> **Railway Signals.**
> One pull of the bell cord signifies "stop."
> Two pulls mean "go ahead."
> Three pulls mean "back up."
> One whistle signifies "downbrakes."
> Two whistles signify "off brakes."
> Three whistles mean "back up."
> Continued whistles indicate "danger."
> Short rapid whistles, "a cattle alarm."
> A sweeping parting of the hands on a level with the eyes means "go ahead."
> A slowly sweeping meeting of the hands over the head signifies "back slowly."
> A downward motion of the hands, with extended arms, signifies "stop."
> A beckoning motion with one hand indicates "back."
> A red flag waved up the track indicates "danger."
> A red flag by the roadside means "danger ahead."
> A red flag carried on a locomotive signifies "an engine following."
> A red flag raised at a station means "stop."
> A lantern swung at right angles across the track means "stop."
> A lantern raised and lowered vertically is a signal to "start."
> A lantern swung in a circle signifies "back the train."

The patriotic newspaper clippings may have been a mother's way of expressing her anxiety and her pride in her soldier sons.

Notes:

[1] Lydia Rise's Album:

Publisher:	Moss & Brother, Publishers, Philadelphia
Dimensions:	9½ X 7¼ inches
Covers:	Brown leather over boards. Gilt-stamped "THE FLORAL ALBUM" on the front cover and "ALBUM" on the spine.
Pages:	Title Page "ALBUM" with color lithograph floral surround. Moss & Brother, Publishers, Philadelphia. White pages, some with color full-page floral lithographs.
First entry:	1856

[2] Ancestry.com: Samuel Rise
Born 1811, Lebanon, PA Died 1850, Lebanon, PA
Married in 1837 to Julianna Good 1823 -1885

[3] Ancestry.com: US Census 1860 Lebanon, Lebanon County, PA lists
Juliana Rise 37, hotel keeper
Henry Rise 17 machinist apprentice
George Rise 15
Lydia Rise 14 (later the album's owner)
Adam Rise 13

[4] Ancestry.com: Civil War Soldier records and profiles. Henry G. Rise enlisted Company K, Pennsylvania 93rd infantry Oct 13, 1861.

[5] Mark, Penrose G. *Red, White, and Blue Badge, Pennsylvania Veteran Volunteers, a History of The 93rd Regiment Known As the Lebanon Infantry.* Harrisburg, Pennsylvania. The Aughinbaugh Press, 1911.

[6] Linton, Charles (1828-1886). *The Healing of the Nations.* (A twenty-two- year-old blacksmith tells the story of the writing of the poem *Our National Ensign* under the influence of the young spiritualist Mary Cunningham.) New York Society for the Diffusion of Spiritual Knowledge, 1855

[7] Wikipedia: Luther C. Ladd.

[8] Fort Wright was at one time the northernmost Confederate position on the Mississippi. The Union gunboat bombardment occurred on April 19, 1862.

[9] McGinty, Brian. . (Details the episode of *THE S.J.WARING.*) *The Rest I Will Kill.* W.W. Norton & Co. 2017

[10] Ancestry.com: US Census 1870 Lebanon, PA. Adam Rise, 22, brakeman.

[11] Ancestry.com: Lydia A Rise
Birth about 1846 Lebanon, PA
Residence 1866, San Francisco, CA.
Death Aug 29, 1876 at Red Cloud agency, Dawes County, Nebraska. Burial Nov 4, 1876 "Husband had traveled with her corpse and corpse of one three-year-old female child for burial at his new duty station in Omaha."

[12] Proceeding and Addresses of the Pennsylvania German Society, 1893.

[13] Ancestry.com: San Francisco City Directory entries 1867 thru 1882.

CHAPTER 9
THE SOUTHERN MARSEILLAISE

VERNON RHODES' Common Place Book:
Title on spine

The Commonplace Book[1] used by a Memphis, Tennessee family to record topics of interest includes a handwritten copy of a stirring Confederate anthem, *The Southern Marseillaise*.

> "*Sons of the South, awake to glory*
> *A thousand voices bid you rise! .....*"
>
> by A.E. Blackmar New Orleans, 1862

The book reveals much about the Rhodes family's cultural interests. The owner was also an enthusiastic inventor.

THE BOOK & ITS OWNER

- At eight inches by ten inches, and almost four hundred pages, the book is large by comparison with other albums.
- It is full of handwritten notes of information and poetry collected by the owner(s), together with an index.
- Included is a handwritten transcription of the patriotic song of the Confederacy, *The Southern Marseillaise*.

VERNON RHODES' Common Place Book 1838

In the more than two hundred pages of handwritten entries, there are few clues in the book to the owner's identity. A pencil note on one page includes the names of a Miss Katie Rhodes and a Mrs. Vernon Rhodes. The written dates range from 1838 to 1863. One of the few place names noted is Germantown, Tennessee, a city close to Memphis.

It appears that the book was used by the Rhodes family for a period of at least twenty-five years starting in about 1838. At that time, according to later census records, Vernon Rhodes would have been nineteen years old and Sallie would have been nine or ten. It seems probable that Vernon was the original owner. US Census records for the years 1870[2] and 1880[3] list only one Vernon Rhodes in Tennessee, living in Shelby County, which included Memphis and Germantown. The family, as listed in the census for 1880, included wealthy cotton merchant Vernon Rhodes, aged 61, his wife Sallie, aged 51, with two sons and a twenty-four-year-old daughter Katy.

COMMONPLACE BOOKS

During the early decades of the nineteenth century, blank notebooks were used mostly to record or copy in the handwriting of the owner, information that he or she deemed worth preserving. The phrase "Common Place Book" was frequently applied to such books, and that term was sometimes marked on the cover or spine. The written entries would, in some instances, start in the handwriting of the owner, only to have additional material added by others at the owner's invitation; in this way they evolved into being used as autograph albums. By the 1830s, books were being sold for this latter purpose with the title *ALBUM*.

The spine of Vernon Rhodes' book is marked in gilt lettering:

LOCKE'S
COMMON PLACE
BOOK.

The title page lists publishers Cummings & Hilliard of Boston, with a publication date of 1822.

A

COMMON PLACE BOOK,

UPON THE PLAN RECOMMENDED AND PRACTISED BY

JOHN LOCKE, ESQ.

There is no need I should tell you, how useful it has been to me, after five and twenty years' experience.

LOCKE'S LETTER TO M. TOIGNARD.

BOSTON:
PUBLISHED BY CUMMINGS AND HILLIARD,
AND FOR SALE AT THEIR
BOOKSTORES IN BOSTON AND CAMBRIDGE.
1822.

VERNON RHODES' Common Place Book, title page

The opening pages of the book include a printed explanation of how to create an index according to a system devised by the eighteenth century English philosopher John Locke[4]. The pages of the book were to be numbered, and index pages, one for the initial letter of every topic, were divided into six parts, labeled with the five vowels plus the letter "y." Topic names were placed in the blocks according to the initial letter and the first vowel of the word, along with the page number.

A.

a ATTRACTION, 10. ART, 13.	*o* ATMOSPHERE, 15.
e AMERICA, 11.	*u* AUTHORITY, 12.
i AIR, 14, 17.	*y* ARMY, 16.

Locke's indexing system illustrated in
VERNON RHODES' Common Place Book

The handwritten contents of this example represent a wide range of interests, as well as prose and poetry copied from various sources. Topics include astronomy, cheerfulness, disappointment, God, history, kindness, life, passion, providence, religion, riches, temper, and time. In many instances the source of the entry is listed by name. The page number for each subject is entered in the index according to Locke's directions.

Copied into the book are numerous examples of verse mostly from British poets, including, among others, Robert Burns, Lord Byron, John Milton, and William Shakespeare. Only one American poet is included, Mrs. David Porter. The poetry is, for the most part, not indexed.

THE CIVIL WAR

The place name found on some pages "Germantown, Tennessee," with dates from 1862 and 1863, suggests that Rhodes family was in the Memphis area during the Civil War.

A brief gunboat battle in the Mississippi River on July 6^{th,} 1862, resulted in the Confederates abandoning the city[5]. With its railroad connections, Memphis became an important supply depot for the Union troops. The Memphis and Charleston Railroad ran through Germantown, and the Union Army sacked and burned the town when they built a fort to protect their own supply lines.

It was about this time that the book's owner wrote in longhand the words of a patriotic song that stands out in contrast with most of the other entries. The anthem's inclusion in the album testifies to the Confederate sentiments of the Rhodes family.

THE SOUTHERN MARSEILLAISE

The French anthem, originally called *The War Song of the Rhine Army,* was written by a French officer, when in 1792 during the French Revolution, France declared war against Austria. Sung by volunteers from Marseilles and soon known as *La Marseillaise*, the song was first adopted as national anthem in 1795. In France it was banned for parts of the nineteenth century and officially reinstated in 1879.

In 1820 the English poet Percy Bysshe Shelly wrote an English translation, loosely based on the French original, to be sung in time with the music of the French original, starting with the lines:

> *Ye sons of France, awake to glory*
> *Hark, hark, what myriads bid you rise!*

The refrain reads:

> *March on! March on!*
> *All hearts resolved*
> *On victory or death.*

Shelley's translation became the basis for a war-song for the Confederacy, *The Southern Marsellaise*, written in 1861 by a New Orleans music publisher, Armand E. Blackmar[6], and intended to be sung to the same tune as the French anthem.

Blackmar, from Bennington, Vermont, moved to New Orleans to teach music, and he and his brother Henry established a music publishing business there. With the onset of the Civil War Armand wrote and distributed songs dedicated to the Southern cause. He was such an enthusiastic supporter of the Confederacy that he named his daughter Louisianna Rebel "Lulu" Blackmar. When New Orleans fell to Union forces in 1862, it was declared that anyone caught singing Southern patriotic songs would be charged with treason. The Blackmar brothers moved the publishing business to Atlanta, but Armand stayed in New Orleans and was eventually arrested and fined. Armand Blackmar is known today primarily for his contributions to the game of chess; an expert player, he originated what became known as the Blackmar gambit.

The *Southern Marsellaise* appealed first to the French-speaking population of southern Louisiana, and its popularity spread quickly.

The first verse, handwritten in the album, is a call to action:

Sons of the South, awake to glory
A thousand voices bid you rise!
Your children, wives and grandsires hoary
Gaze on you now with trusting eyes!
Your country every strong arm calling,
To meet the hireling Northern band
That comes to desolate the land
With fire and blood and scenes appalling,
To arms, to arms, ye brave!
Th'avenging sword unsheathe!

The reference to "grandsires hoary" seems to be a poetic stretch, but Blackmar evidently adopted the phrase from Shelley's translation. The refrain continues:

March on! March on!
All hearts resolved
On victory or death.

The second verse, with its dire warnings of invasion by the Union forces, would have struck home with family living in Memphis and so close to the military action...

Now, now the dangerous storm is rolling
Which treacherous Brothers madly raise,
The dogs of war let loose are howling
And soon our peaceful towns may blaze,
Shall friends who basely plot our ruin
Unchecked advance with guilty stride
To spread destruction far and wide,
With Southrons' blood their hands embruing.

"Southron[7]" was a term for a person living in the south. "Embruing" means "staining". To avoid harassment by the Union authorities, Blackmar frequently used pseudonyms when signing his songs, including A. Noir, Ye Comic, and A. Southron. The third stanza contains a commentary on the political backdrop.

> *With needy, starving mobs surrounded*
> *The jealous, blind fanatics dare*
> *To offer, in their zeal unbounded*
> *Our happy slaves, their tender care.*
> *The South, though deepest wrongs bewailing*
> *Long yielded all to Union's name,*
> *But Independence now we claim,*
> *And all their threats are unavailing.*

The reference to "Our happy slaves" reflects an interesting point of view about slavery!

VERNON RHODES THE INVENTOR

Vernon Rhodes was not only a successful merchant, but his financial resources enabled him to indulge a creative urge. He and one of his sons are credited with patents for several inventions, none of which appear to have achieved commercial success.

In 1879, the son, Webster Nazer Rhodes, patented a churn driven by a clockwork mechanism.[8] His father was one of the two witnesses who signed the patent document.

Vernon Rhodes was awarded two patents for agricultural devices. His 1888 invention of a "cultivator"[9] was a rake with a gap in the middle for cultivating two rows at a time. His 1891 invention for "Perforated Blade for Plows, &c."[10] was a ploughshare, with holes cut through the blade, which he claimed would more thoroughly prepare soil for planting.

His most extraordinary patent was for a chamber pot, invented in 1870, U.S. Patent 110,286. Its novel feature is a vertical partition dividing the pot into two compartments. Rhodes claimed that, "in the sick room, the physician will be enabled to examine the discharged fecal matter and urine separately, and thereby, in a majority of cases, to trace the cause of the complaint of his patient, a result which is unobtainable by the use of the ordinary chamber-vessel". The inventor was sufficiently confident of the future commercial success of his invention that he even filed through an agent for a British patent.[11] There is no evidence of the device being commercially produced or marketed.

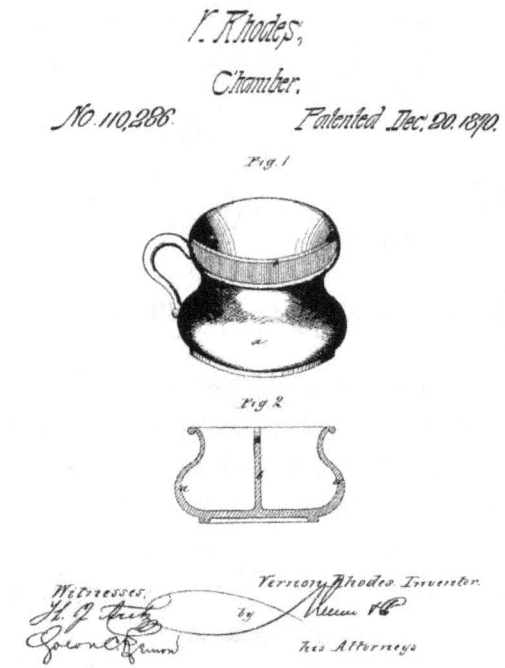

U.S. Patent 110,286 for a "Chamber": invented by Vernon Rhodes of Memphis, Tennessee.

That Vernon Rhodes survived the Civil War, with his wealth sufficiently intact, so as to be able to pursue invention as a hobby was quite remarkable.

Notes:

[1] Vernon Rhodes's Album:

    Publisher: Cummings & Hilliard, Boston

    Dimensions: 10 X 8 inches

    Covers: Marbled paper over boards, with leather spine. . Gilt-stamped "LOCKE'S COMMON PLACE BOOK" on the spine.

    Pages: Title page COMMON PLACE BOOK UPON THE PLAN RECOMMENDED AND PRACTISED BY JOHN LOCKE ESQ... Published by Cummings & Hilliard, Boston 1822

    First entry: 1838

[2] Ancestry.com: US Census 1870.

[3] Ancestry.com: US Census 1880.

[4] Wikipedia: English philosopher John Locke's book *A New Method for Making Common-Place Books, London,* 1706.

[5] Wikipedia: First Battle of Memphis.1862

[6] Wikipedia: Armand Edward Blackmar was born in Vermont in 1826.

[7] Southron: a person from the South, or Southerner, especially the Southern United States.

[8] US Patent 222,076: "Improvement in Machinery for Operating Churns."

[9] US Patent 381,169: "Cultivator."

[10] US Patent 447,437: "Perforated Blade for Plows".

[11] British Patent 2,634: "An Improved Chamber Utensil." Reported in *The London Gazette*, October 14, 1870. Filed by Alfred Vincent Newton, patent agent.

CHAPTER 10
The "Seed Corn" of the Confederacy

ELLA McQUEEN'S album 1858

The death of one of the "boy-soldiers[1]" recruited by the Confederacy in the last year of the Civil War was reported in a newspaper clipping that was pasted into the album[2] of the soldier's cousin Ella McQueen. Additional clippings of obituaries provide details of more of Ella's cousins, who were from the same Scottish enclave of North Carolina, and who died for the Southern cause.

THE ALBUM

The first page of the album is inscribed:

> *Miss Ella McQueen, November 15th, 1858*

Below her name is written in a different hand:

> *My grandmother (maternal) died at the time Mother was born. ECB*

Ella was sixteen years old when she received the *BOUDOIR ALBUM*. Many of the inscriptions include place-names in Robeson County, southeastern North Carolina, adjacent to the South Carolina State line. Some list educational institutions that Ella attended:

- Floral Academy near Maxton in Robeson County: the first college for women in North Carolina to confer degrees.
- St. Mary's, Raleigh N.C.: was a highly regarded preparatory school.

One of Ella's classmates left a woven hair token in the album; the page is stained by oils from the hair.

Entry in ELLA McQUEEN'S album with a woven hair insert

Annabella McCallum, author of the family history, *The MacQueens of Queensdale*, which was published in 1916[3], signed "Your affectionate cousin Bella McCallum."

THE CONFEDERATE JUNIOR RESERVES

Faced with a desperate imbalance in the number of soldiers that the Confederate States Army could field against the North, the Confederate Congress in February 1864 passed a law which extended the ages range for military service. Males aged seventeen to eighteen years could be placed in reserve.

The move led to much soul searching among the southern leadership. The President of the Confederate States, Jefferson Davis, was said to have used the term "a robbing of the cradle" when formation of the Junior Reserves[4] was approved by the Confederate Congress. Of the plan to risk the lives of these youngest men, North Carolina Governor Zebulon Vance used the term "grinding up the seed corn of the Confederacy.[5]"

After a short period in which the younger men were permitted to volunteer, in April and May of 1864 seventeen-year-olds were being conscripted into State Reserve battalions and sent to training camps of instruction. One such destination was in Wilmington, where the Seventh Battalion[6], comprising three companies was formed on June 4th 1864 with a Major William Foster French as field officer.

WILMINGTON, NORTH CAROLINA

From the beginning of the Civil War, Union forces blockaded Southern ports. The city of Wilmington, located thirty miles upstream from the mouth of the Cape Fear River, became one of the most important locations for importing goods to the Confederacy, primarily from the British Caribbean colonies.

Early during the War, normal quarantine arrangements in some ports were sometimes waived for blockade running ships. That changed in the summer of 1862 after yellow fever spread from infected sailors aboard the English vessel Kate[7] which arrived in Wilmington from Nassau. The epidemic afflicted two thousand people and led to stricter procedures. Nevertheless the city, with the large influx of sailors, continued to experience bouts of contagious diseases.

The port's river-mouth defenses at Fort Fisher were exceptionally robust, and their protection became a Confederate priority. It was therefor to Wilmington that a Regiment of the Junior Reserves were sent for training in picket and guard duty on the beaches to prevent infiltration of enemies and the escape of slaves.

THE ALBUM – NEWSPAPER CLIPPINGS

Pasted into the pages are three obituary notices from *The Fayetteville* (NC) *Observer*, the newspaper which served Robeson and adjacent counties. All three were for young Confederate officers who were also cousins of Ella. When Ella first used the album, her close neighbor Donald "Donnie" McQueen was ten years old. Seven years later, he volunteered for the Junior Reserves and traveled to Wilmington for training. His obituary reads, in part:

> At the residence of Mr. Alex Sprunt, in Wilmington, on the morning of the 16th ult[8]. After a brief but painful illness of five days, Capt. DONALD McQUEEN, son of Col. A.J. and Caroline McQueen of Richmond county, in the 17th year of his age. In obedience to orders received the deceased, in common with others of his age from the 4th Congressional District, just two weeks previous repaired to Wilmington for the purpose of being organized into companies for State defence. Without opposition and by a unanimous vote, he was chosen Captain of Company C,

French's Battalion of Junior Reserves. Donnie was a noble boy in the fullest sense of the word. …

> At the residence of Mr. Alex. Sprunt, in Wilmington, on the morning of the 16th ult., after a brief but painful illness of five days, Capt. DONALD McQUEEN, son of Col. A. J. and Caroline M Queen, of Richmond county in the 17th year of his age. In obedience to orders received the deceased, in common with others of his age from the 4th Congressional District, just two weeks previous, repaired to Wilmington for the purpose of being organized into companies for State defence. Without opposition, and by a unanimous vote, he was chosen Captain of Company C, French's Battalion of Junior Reserves. With a mind well disciplined for a youth of his age, and a disposition always frank, open-hearted and generous, he soon endeared himself to all his young comrades in arms, exhibiting during the few days he was permitted to stay with them, an entire devotedness to the comfort, the convenience and the best interests of his company. And the deep anxiety with which they watched over him in his illness, and the many bitter tears they shed around his lifeless remains, bore ample testimony to the strong mutual love and mutual confidence that had sprung up between them. But he has fallen in the bloom of his youth and in the brightness of his promise, and his precious name added to the long galaxy of youthful martyrs, whose lives have been offered as fragrant oblations upon the altar of their bleeding country. Donnie was a noble boy in the fullest sense of the word. Modest and unassuming as a child, firm and resolute as a man, sincere and truthful in all the relations of life, he won the love and respect of all who knew him, and a bright and honored prospect loomed up before him.

Two more of the death notices were for Ella's cousins killed in battle:

Lt. J.B. Morrison of Robeson county N.C. was killed instantly near Spottsylvania C.H.[9] on the 5th of May in his 22nd year. He entered the Confederate service in May 1861, was wounded at Hanover C.H.[10] in May 1862. …

> Lt. J. B. MORRISON, of Robeson county, N. C., was killed instantly, near Spottsylvania C. H., on the 8th of May, in his 22d year. He entered the Confederate service in May 1861, was wounded at Hanover C. H., in May 1862. In October, 1863, he connected himself with the Presbyterian church, and has since given the most consoling evidence to his friends that he was a child of God—an Israelite indeed in whom there was no guile. His letters written a short time before his death to a widowed mother, evince not only the fondness of his filial love, but breathe full of a pure spirit of piety. This is the second stroke for that weeping mother; a few months ago the partner of her bosom; now the next natural support, her first-born son; is gone. But let her not mourn as those without hope. A patriot has only fallen at the post of duty; a child of God, we trust, has only gone home to his rest. — FRIEND.

Lieut. Jas B McCallum died on the battlefield of Drewry's Bluff[11] on the 16th of May, from wounds received 4 hours previous. He was a native of Robeson county, 2d Lieutenant Co. D Fifty-first NC Reg't, a graduate of the University of NC. …

> FOR THE OBSERVER.
> Lieut Jas B McCallum died on the battle-field of Drewry's Bluff on the 16th of May, from wounds received 4 hours previous. He was a native of Robeson county, 2d Lieutenant Co D, Fifty-first N C Reg't, a graduate of the University of N C and for a short while a student in Columbia Theological Seminary, but he felt as if he was needed in the awful strife for independence and he left the peaceful walls of the Seminary to take his stand with others of N Carolina's brave sons to battle for his loved country. And nobly did he do his duty: he participated in the fight of Goldsboro, the assault of Battery Wagner, and the bloody battle of Drewry's Bluff, from whence his beloved God saw fit to call him from such scenes of blood and carnage to a bright celestial home above. Oh! it is heartrending to think of the many noble youths who have cheerfully given themselves to their country; but a nobler, truer, braver patriot has never lived the life or died the death of a soldier than the subject of this brief notice.

THE McQUEENS OF QUEENSDALE

Family tradition has it that the McQueens proudly trace their origins back to King Robert the Bruce of Scotland. In *The MacQueens of Queensdale*, Bella McCallum the author of the clan history, wrote about Colonel James McQueen (1760-1824), the common ancestor of the McQueens of Robeson County[12].

Colonel James McQueen 1760-1824

James McQueen was born on the Isle of Skye; his mother was the half-sister of the Scottish Jacobite heroine Flora MacDonald. About the year 1772, McQueen arrived at the North Carolina port of Wilmington. He was part of the wave of Scottish immigrants who arrived in the New World fleeing religious persecution. In 1790 he married another Scottish immigrant, Ann McRae. A few years after their marriage, the couple set up home in Robeson County and

> ... founded the Queensdale homestead, purchasing government and other lands to the extent of several hundred acres, and erecting a house, elegant in its day, and noted for lavish hospitality.[13]

Ella's father, James Hugh McQueen, born in 1808, was the fifth, and last, son of Colonel James McQueen and his wife. A farmer who succeeded in accumulating considerable wealth, he established

> ... a large landed estate one mile from Queensdale, and a fine homestead, which he called Circlewood. ... His home was finely furnished, in suites of elegant mahogany, and heavy silverware, much of which was mutilated and destroyed during the War Between the States, by General Sherman's raiders. He was an energetic businessman, and was one of the pioneers of the cotton factory industry in this country ...[13]

Ella's mother died when Ella and her sister Annie were young, and James Hugh McQueen never remarried.

> With the aid of a devoted slave woman he raised the children to maturity ... They received the best educational advantages that the State afforded at that day, having spent several sessions at Floral College[14]. They were subsequently graduated from St. Mary's College, Raleigh, N.C. and were among the most accomplished young ladies of this section.

Ella McQueen, the album's owner, was described by the McQueen biographer, Bella McCallum, as

> ... *about medium height, with slender graceful figure, light hair, blue eyes, and features of classic beauty and regularity. In her manner were a winning grace and natural ease and dignity I have never seen surpassed.*[13]

Ella's father was one of twelve siblings, and in consequence Ella had numerous cousins. One of her father's sisters, Catherine McQueen (1796 – 1862), married a Donald McQueen, who, despite his surname, was not related in any way to his wife or her family. He was

> ... *a native-born Scot, .who spoke the Gaelic tongue, sang Scotch songs, and was doubtless a Highlander. ... a man of gigantic physical proportions.*[13]

Colonel Donald McQueen

Donald "Donnie" McQueen, cousin to Ella, the Junior Reserve soldier, whose obituary was pasted into the album, was a grandson of this Catherine and Donald McQueen.

ELLA McQUEEN'S DESCENDANTS

In 1866, when she was twenty-four years of age, Ella married Confederate veteran Thomas Benson Ledbetter[15]; Thomas was a forty-one year-old factory-owner, engaged in the cotton-mill business. The couple had two sons, Henry and James, and a daughter Mary Benson Ledbetter, who was born in 1872, shortly before Ella died at thirty years of age.

Mary was the "mother" referred to in the note on the first page of the album. She married tobacco farmer, Rawlins Desha Best[16] in 1895; their only child, Eleanor Campbell Best (1903 – 1991), was the "ECB" who wrote in the album the note about her grandmother Ella McQueen.

The album escaped the destruction that occurred when General Sherman's Army made its scorched-earth march through the Carolinas in the spring of 1865. By being passed down through Ella's daughter and granddaughter, the book survived to the present day.

Notes:

[1] http://www.ncpedia.org/north-carolina%E2%80%99s-youngest-soldiers

[2] Ella McQueen's Album:

Publisher:	Hayes & Zell, Philadelphia
Dimensions:	8 X 6 ½ inches
Covers:	Black leather over boards, with leather spine. . Gilt-stamped "BOUDOIR ALBUM" on the front and back covers and "ALBUM" on spine.
Pages:	Title page "BOUDOIR ALBUM" Philadelphia HAYES & ZELL.
First entry:	1858

[3] MacElyea, Annabella Bunting. *The MacQueens of Queensdale*. Published by the Committee of Publication of the Clan McQueen 1916.

[4] Clark, Walter. *Histories of the Several Regiments and Battalions from North Carolina in the Great War 1861–'65.* State of North Carolina, Vol. 4, 1904.

[5] Pearce, Jordan. *Grinding up the Seed Corn of the Confederacy: The North Carolina Junior Reserves.* East Carolina University, 2013. http://uncw.edu/csurf/Explorations/Volume%20XI/Pearce.pdf

[6] *Fayetteville Observer*: Jun 16, 1864 "The following is the organization of the 7th Battalion, Junior Reserves recently called out from this district." From the *Wilmingon Journal*. Included was Donald McQueen, Capt. Company C.

[7] The story that the infection arrived with the steamer *Kate* has been challenged by later researchers. http://www.ncpedia.org/history/health/yellow-ever

[8] "ult" is an archaic term for "last month".

[9] Wikipedia: Battle of Spottsylvania, VA Court House May 8 – 21, 1864.

[10] Wikipedia: Battle of Hanover, VA Court House May 27, 1862.

[11] Wikipedia: Battle of Drewry's Bluff, VA May 15, 1864.

[12] *The MacQueens of Queensdale* page14

[13] *The MacQueens of Queensdale*

[14] Floral College, in Maxton NC, was founded in 1841 by John Gilchrist, Jr. and closed in 1878.

[15] Ancestry.com: Ella McQueen married Thomas Benson Ledbetter Sep 6, 1866

[16] Ancestry.com: Mary Benson Ledbetter married Rawlins Desha Best Oct 3, 1895

CHAPTER 11
THE IMMORTAL SIX HUNDRED

Memorial at Fort Pulaski, Georgia

Confederate Colonel Dorilas Henry Lee Martz, husband of the owner of the shown on the next page, was involved in events that became known as the story of "The Immortal Six Hundred."

To the victor in war comes the privilege of writing the story of the conflict, and the opportunity to reflect well on the winner and badly on the loser. In histories of the American Civil War, accounts of the appalling conditions to which prisoners of war were exposed most often cite Andersonville, the camp maintained by Confederate forces in Andersonville, Georgia for captured enlisted Union soldiers. In fact, there were terrible examples on both sides of inhumane treatment of POW's.

THE ALBUM

MOLLIE CARTER'S album 1859

The first entries in Mollie Carter's album[1] date from the years 1859 and 1860. She was attending Rockingham County (Virginia) Female Institute, when her friends and relatives wrote in her book. One was a love poem, from a suitor whom she did not in fact marry.

>
> *To Miss Mollie*
> *I Think of Thee*
> *I think of thee when evening's ray*
> *Is glancing o'er the sea*
> *When gentle twilight shadows play*
> *On mountain vale and tree.*
> *That sweet fair form and cheek of rose*
> *Those lips with fragrance wet;*
> *All, all thy joy's youth disclose –*
> *Maiden I see thee yet.*
> *Harrisburg August 2nd, '59.*
> *John W. Houck*

MOLLIE CARTER

Mary Mollie Nicholas Carter[2] was born in 1838 to Nancy Carter and her wealthy husband, farmer Richard Carter of Albemarle County, Virginia.

MOLLIE CARTER MARTZ

In November 1860, Mollie married twenty-three-year-old merchant Dorilas Henry Lee Martz. They had four children, only two of whom survived past infancy, daughter Nannie Lee and son Edward Carter Martz[3].

The album has many attempts by the little girl to copy the writings of the adults, and this cartoon of a man and woman, in period dress, dancing.

The family's black housemaid, Ella Vern also wrote several times in the album at this time, as did Willamette Sprinkel, daughter of Mollie's married sister Sallie.

DORILAS MARTZ

Martz's German immigrant ancestors[4] arrived in Maryland in the 1700s, and by the early 1800s prospered as farmers in Rockingham County in neighboring Virginia. Dorilas Martz's life is summarized in his 1914 obituary[5]:

> *He was born March 23, 1837. His father Hiram Martz was a member of the Virginia House of delegates for four terms prior to the War Between the States.*
>
> *The early life of Colonel Martz was spent on the farm, after which he engaged in the mercantile business in Harrisonburg. In 1859 he became a member of the Valley Guards, a militia organized in the latter fifties, and as orderly sergeant he accompanied the organization to Charlestown, Virginia, where it was a part of the guard at the trial and execution of John Brown, the Kansas abolitionist.*

TO WAR

When the call for Confederate volunteers came in 1861, Rockingham County's Valley Guards formed the nucleus of the Tenth Virginia Infantry Regiment. Seven of the eleven companies that made up the Tenth Virginia were drawn from Rockingham County. A total of about 1,350 men served in the Tenth during the time when the regiment was under arms. As part of the Army of Northern Virginia, the regiment saw action in almost every major engagement that was fought in Virginia, Maryland and Pennsylvania.

Four brothers from the Martz family went to war at the same time, Addison Martz and his younger siblings Dorilas, Daniel and Michael. All but the oldest survived. Dorilas was soon promoted to lieutenant and then to captain of his company. His co-captain was his brother-in-law Charles A. Sprinkel; one of the Company's lieutenants was John W. Houck, the rejected suitor who before the war had written the love poem for Mollie Carter's album.

Martz's obituary[5] describes his military service:

> He first saw action in the Battle of McDowell in May 1862, then the First Battle of Winchester, the Seven Days Battles around Richmond, then Cedar Mountain and Second Manassas. In May 1863, at Chancellorsville he was wounded and had not recovered from his injuries when the Battle of Gettysburg took place in July. After Chancellorsville he was promoted to lieutenant colonel. In the battles near Petersburg in early May 1864, his colonel and major were killed leaving Martz the only field officer of the regiment. On May 12th, at the battle of Spotsylvania Courthouse, nearly all of the regiment were captured, including Martz, and sent to Fort Delaware, on Pea Patch Island in the Delaware River.

PRISONER OF WAR

Fort Delaware was created originally to defend the entrance to the Delaware River and the approaches to Wilmington, Delaware and Philadelphia. It was constructed on a marshy island in the middle of the river near the entrance to Delaware Bay. When it was adapted by the Union Army to house prisoners of war, wooden barracks were constructed for most of the prison population, the enlisted men and junior officers (mostly lieutenants and captains). Higher-ranking officers had quarters inside the fort. Here Dorilas Martz spent a few weeks after his capture before being transported with fifty other officers south to Charleston, South Carolina.

During the War, the Union Forces blockaded southern port cities to prevent supplies from reaching the Confederates. By the summer of 1863, Federal heavy artillery was positioned at Fort Wagner on Morris Island at the entrance to Charleston Harbor, four miles from the city, which was still in Confederate hands. Union forces started a bombardment that would last through the next year. The Confederates responded by shelling the Union batteries. The Confederate general commanding Charleston placed fifty Union officer prisoners in a home in a part of the city that was under fire, and communicated this fact to his opposite Union number. This action set off a chain of events, of which the first was the sending fifty Confederate officer prisoners south from Fort Delaware, with the threat that they would be used as human shields in a camp to be constructed in front of the guns on Morris Island. Colonel Dorilas Martz was one of these fifty officers who faced the threat of being used in this way.

PRISONER EXCHANGES

In April 1863, the Federal Government, in order to prevent soldiers from returning to the ranks of the Southern armies, had ended a practice of exchanging prisoners of like rank. General U.S. Grant was said to have argued, "It was cheaper to feed rebel prisoners than to fight them." The result was a rapid swelling of the numbers in both Southern and Northern prisons, and a resulting deterioration in conditions for captives.

Advised of the situation in Charleston, President Lincoln authorized an exception to policy. Before the fifty Confederate officers were actually placed on Morris Island, the exchange took place. On August 3rd, 1864, Dorilas Martz was released and returned to his regiment, and so narrowly avoided the fate of many more of his Confederate fellow officers.

THE IMMORTAL SIX HUNDRED

For a number of for Martz's fellow officer, the exchange of the fifty prisoners was not, however, the end of the episode. General Sherman's march across Georgia was getting close to the overcrowded camp at Andersonville, and the Confederates moved some prisoners to Charleston. When the Union commander heard of this movement of captives, he assumed that the Confederates planned to use them as human shields. In retaliation and with the approval of Edwin M. Stanton, the Secretary of War, he ordered six-hundred Confederate officers to be removed from Fort Delaware and shipped to Morris Island. On August 20th, 1864 the paddle wheel steamer *Crescent City*, with the Confederate prisoners jammed into its hold, left Pea Patch Island in the hot summer sun.

The six-hundred included one hundred and seventy-three who were captured on May 12th at Spotsylvania Courthouse at the same time as Dorilas Martz, including seven officers from Martz's regiment. The prisoners stayed for two weeks on the *Crescent City* near Hilton Head while the stockade on Morris Island was being completed. Once on the island, the captives endured forty-five days with shells from both sides passing overhead. Some of the Union guards were injured by falling shrapnel, but miraculously none of the prisoners were killed.

On October 21st, the Confederate officers were moved to Fort Pulaski at Savannah, Georgia, where they spent a miserable winter, thirteen dying of disease. These dead are commemorated on a plaque at Fort Pulaski. In March 1865 the remaining prisoners were shipped back to Fort Delaware, where twenty-five more died. They remained there until the war ended; the last man was not released until July.

The name "The Immortal Six Hundred" was coined by one of the captives, John O. Murray, as the title of a first-hand account of the episode[6]. In addition to the volume published in 1905, two recent books tell the men's stories, *Immortal Captives*[7] published in 1996, and from 2013, *The Immortal 600 – Surviving Civil War Charleston and Savannah*[8].

DORILAS MARTZ AFTER THE WAR

After the war, Martz returned to business in Rockingham County[9] as a merchant. By 1875 he was appointed deputy clerk of the County Court and in 1887 was elected circuit clerk, an office to which he was re-elected by the unanimous choice of the voters.

Colonel Dorilas Henry Martz

Colonel Martz's son Edward became a respected lawyer. Daughter Nannie Lee, who had scribbled in the album, married a publisher, who later turned electrician.

When the Harrisonburg chapter of the United Confederate Veterans organization was organized in 1893, Martz became its first Commander. For the book *A History of Rockingham County*[10], published in 1912, Colonel Martz was asked to contribute a chapter about the Tenth Virginia Regiment, Volunteer Infantry. His account of being captured, imprisoned and exchanged is limited to the following:

> On the 12th of May, General Hancock, of the Federals, made his famous assault on our works, capturing nearly all of Johnson's Division, including the 10th Virginia and the writer.

Of his release Martz said:

> The writer was exchanged on the 3rd of August, 1864, came home and rejoined his command. In the meantime, however, the regiment was no bigger than a Company.

Regarding the end of the War he remarked:

On the morning of April 9 we had a skirmish with the enemy at Appomattox, driving them some distance, only to be withdrawn and to furl our banners, - banners never again to be unfurled. But the Tenth did not surrender the old battle flag, which was hidden under the coat of the one remaining lieutenant who commanded just 8 or 10 muskets. The writer had been put in charge of the 10th, 23d and 37th regiments. Here ended the military career of the noble Tenth Virginia. By April 15 we were home again to start life anew.

Martz's account of his imprisonment and release was written fifty years after the fact. He wrote in some detail about the military actions during the War and the officers involved, but he omitted completely any references to the conditions for prisoners of war. He also avoided the subject of being sent to Hilton Head and to Morris Island to be used as a human shield. No doubt he was well aware of the story of "The Immortal 600," after all seven of the men were from the Tenth Virginia, but his account of his regiment's history makes no mention of their ordeal. For a man in an important public office in a state close to Washington D.C., it may not have been smart to emphasize the actions of a Federal Government which had conducted policies of using of human shields and retaliation against prisoners of war.

Notes:

[1] Mollie Carter's Album:

Publisher:	Moss & Brother, Philadelphia
Dimensions:	7 ¾ X 6 inches
Covers:	Brown leather over boards. Gilt-stamped "THE TABLET OF FRIENDSHIP" with classical / floral frame on front cover and "ALBUM" on spine.
Pages:	Title Page "FRIENDSHIP'S TABLET". Moss & Bro., PA Pastel pages, some with black & white engravings.
First entry:	1859

[2] Ancestry.com: Louise Clare Herr Burroughs family tree : Mary Mollie Nicholas Carter. Birth: Jul 16, 1838 Albemarle county, VA. Death: Dec 22, 1922, Bridgewater, Rockingham County, Virginia.
Married Nov 14, 1860 Dorilas Henry Lee Martz.
Children:
Julia B Martz 1861 – 1862
Nannie Lee Martz 1866 – 1930
Edward Carter Martz 1867 – 1930
Ernest Martz 1874 - 1875

[3] Ancestry.com: US Census 1870.

[4] Ancestry.com: Colonel Dorilas Henry Lee Martz, Birth: Mar 23, 1837, Rockingham County, VA Death: Oct 20, 1914, Harrisonburg, Virginia.

[5] http://www.confederatevets.com/documents/martz_va_cv_02_15_ob.shtml

[6] Murray, Major Ogden. *The Immortal Six Hundred A Story of Cruelty to Confederate Prisoners*. The Eddy Press, Winchester Virginia, 1905.

[7] Joslyn, Mauriel Phillips. *Immortal Captives*. White Mane Publishing Co. Shippensburg, Pennsylvania,1996

[8] Stokes, Karen. *The Immortal 600 – Surviving Civil War Charleston and Savannah*. The History Press, 2013.

[9] Ancestry.com: US Census 1870.

[10] Martz, Colonel D.H. Lee. "Chapter VII, Rockingham in the Civil War 1861 – 1865. A History of the 10th Virginia regiment, Volunteer Infantry." *A History of Rockingham County Virginia*, Ruebush – Elkins, Dayton, Virginia, 1912

CHAPTER 12
THE PIONEER BRIGADE

BESSIE BRAZEE'S album 1879

In 1882, when he signed an inscription in the autograph album[1] of his twelve-year-old daughter Bessie, Christopher Martin Brazee was a man already honored for his achievements. His reputation as a lawyer was acknowledged by his election to the office of City Attorney for Rockford, Illinois. Appointment as Colonel of the local regiment of the Illinois National Guard recognized his extraordinary service at one of the bloodiest battles of the Civil War, the Battle of Stones River at Murfreesboro, Tennessee.

CHRISTOPHER BRAZEE'S MILITARY CAREER

Christopher Brazee grew up in Lockport, Niagara County, New York and studied to be a lawyer. A history of Rockford[2] says,

> In 1856 he joined an engineering corps that was coming to the west. He made his way to Iowa, where he remained in survey and other work for two years, before moving to Rockford to practice law.

The full name for his unit was The Corps of Topographical Engineers, a small but highly significant branch of the Army. According to historian William Goertzmann[3]:

> *The Engineers were concerned with recording all of the western phenomena as accurately as possible, whether main-traveled roads or uncharted wilderness. As Army officers they represented the direct concern of the national government the settling of the West, the Corps of Topographical Engineers was a central institution of Manifest Destiny.*

THE PIONEER BRIGADE

During the year 1863, the Union Army of the Cumberland under General William S. Rosecrans faced off against the Army of Tennessee under Confederate General Braxton Bragg.

One of General Rosecrans' innovations was the creation in November 1862 of the Pioneer Brigade. Two soldiers, volunteers having mechanical skills, were drawn from every company of every regiment. To lead each company of the brigade, a lieutenant from each regiment was selected as "the most intelligent and energetic candidate, with best knowledge of civil engineering." Rosecrans was thus able to assemble a field engineering capability from his own forces without having to turn to Washington for permission.

The brigade was composed mostly of mechanics and laborers, totaling 2,600 men. They were ordered to train in Nashville,

Tennessee for a month and on November 29, 1862 Captain James St. Clair Morton was commissioned to be Brigadier General of the Volunteers.

Brazee was selected to lead one of the companies. His experience with the Topographical Engineers evidently prepared him well for this assignment. *The Annals of the Army of the Cumberland*[4] includes this paragraph:

> *Lieutenant C.M. Brazee, Acting Assistant Quartermaster of the Army. Born in the State of New York in 1831, he settled in Rockford in 1857. Soon after he commenced the study of law, and was admitted to practice in 1859. August 2, 1862 he entered military service and on the 9th of the same month was promoted to first lieutenancy in the 74th Illinois Volunteers. Serving with his regiment in Buell's North Alabama campaign, he was detailed from the regiment with twenty-two men into the Pioneer Brigade, 2nd Battalion, November 30, 1862. Here he was constantly on duty until after the battle of Stones River, when he was sick for some weeks, the result of exposure. On the 8th, February, 1863, he was ordered to report to department headquarters, and assigned to duty upon the staff of General Rosecrans as acting assistant quartermaster.*

THE BATTLE OF STONES RIVER[5]

In December 1862, Confederate forces led by General Bragg occupied the country around Murfreesboro, just south of Nashville; Rosecrans advanced his army from the city for the battle to be remembered as Stones River. About 1,700 men of the Pioneer Brigade joined the rest of the Army of the Cumberland on its march. Arriving on the outskirts of Murfreesboro on the 29th, they were ordered to build bridges, clear roads, improve fords and to construct abatises, obstacles formed, in the modern era, of the branches of trees laid in a row, with the sharpened tops directed outwards, towards the enemy.

During the first day's fighting on December 29th, Bragg surprised Rosecrans by striking first, and the Union forces were pushed into a tight defensive position backing up to the Nashville Turnpike. The Confederates nearly swept the Federals from the field. The struggle continued for two days. In the middle of winter, in freezing conditions, many of the soldiers had to sleep on the ground overnight. A biography of Brigadier Morton, the Brigade's commander,[6] says of the action:

> *On the morning of the 31st, the Pioneer Brigade was positioned to the rear of the Union army. Around mid-day, the men were ordered forward to support a gun battery commanded by Captain James Stokes, which was positioned on a small knoll west of the Nashville Turnpike, behind the center of the Union lines. Upon arriving, they witnessed hundreds of Union soldiers fleeing across the open ground with the Confederate forces reforming for another attack. The Brigade was immediately behind the front lines now and from their position, had a clear view of open meadow in front of them, offering the gun battery a deadly advantage.*
>
> *When the Confederates launched their attack, Morton ordered the cannon to open fire with canister (hollow shells with multiple projectiles), which effectively drove the attackers back.*
>
> *As the front line Union soldiers continued to withdraw, they appeared from the woods directly in front of Morton and then slowly took refuge behind his lines. The Confederates, still in pursuit, began to appear from the woods opposite, allowing Stokes' battery to open fire with canister. Morton rode to the front of his troops and said, 'Men, you haven't much ammunition, but give them what you have and then wade in on 'em with the bayonets!'*
>
> *With that, the lines were ordered to stand and open fire, putting gaps into the oncoming Confederate lines. The Rebels wavered and then began to withdraw. Upon seeing the success of his troops, General Rosecrans ordered the Brigade to charge forward and occupy the fields just outside the woods. The*

Confederates rallied three times and pressed forward again, but each time, were forced back.

As the Pioneer Brigade moved towards the action, the Confederates had already begun retreating, and Morton had his brigade participate in their pursuit. The Confederates withdrew from the city on January 4th, leaving the Union victorious. Morton would report 12 of his Pioneers killed and 23 wounded. In addition, Stokes' battery had 3 killed and 10 wounded. In the entire battle at Murfreesboro, out of about 81,000 soldiers engaged on the two sides, 23,000 were casualties.

Six months after Stones River, Rosecrans began his campaign to drive the Confederates out of Middle Tennessee. In less than two weeks in the summer of 1863, Bragg and his Army were driven all the way back to Chattanooga. The Union forces were positioned for Sherman's March to the Sea in 1864.

BRAZEE, LATER

Brazee was promoted to Captain after he joined Rosecrans' staff in 1863. However, ill health forced him to resign the Army in February 1864.

In Rockford, he resumed his law practice, and was said to be "one the most aggressive advocates who ever practiced at the County bar ... seldom failing to gain the verdict he desired."

In April 1861, he married Lydia Holmes, of Rockford. The couple's first child was Mary Elizabeth, known as Bessie, the owner of the album; she had two sisters and a brother[7]. She was a girl of eight in 1878 when she pasted diecut Victorian stickers into her new album.

In 1883, when Bessie was thirteen, her mother died; three years later Bessie was only sixteen when her father passed away from an illness that lasted three months. Bessie never married; she spent much of her adult life working as a stenographer in Chicago[8]. At seventy-six years of age, she died at Glencoe, Illinois in 1947[9].

STONES RIVER NATIONAL BATTLEFIELD

At Murfreesboro, Tennessee, the National Parks Service today maintains the Stones River National Battlefield site and a military cemetery with more than 6000 graves with Union dead from Stones River and also those re-interred from the Battle of Franklin, which occurred twenty miles away.

Stones River National Battlefield
Murfreesboro, Tennessee

Next to a row of cannon overlooking a slope down a broad meadow is a reproduction of a painting showing men of the illustrious Pioneer Brigade who earlier in the battle had been building bridges and roads, holding the ground to give their comrades cover.

THE PIONEER BRIGADE   147

Stones River National Battlefield:
Memorial to the Pioneer Brigade

The caption to the sign reads:

Stand Fast!
THE PIONEER BRIGADE

On came the sounds of battle .... struggling bluecoats...falling back came into view through the trees. They were loading and firing as the retired...they passed over our...line and laid down behind it. The order 'Battalion, rise up!' came like an electric shock. The brigade was by some mischance short of ammunition, some companies had not more than 20 rounds ... The Confederates were near at hand. Suddenly their line seemed to burst through the thicket just in front. 'Commence firing!' and our volleys were fired into them. Men were dropping here and there, and others filled the vacant places.

Henry Freeman, orderly sergeant, 3rd Battalion, Pioneer Brigade.

The sign goes on to explain:

In the Army of the Cumberland, a brigade of pioneers handled all the army's pick, shovel, and ax work for building roads and bridges.

Officers picked two men from every company of every regiment in the army for this duty. Many of the men who lined up to fight here on this knoll had been carpenters or miners in civilian life. What they had never done before was train to fight as a unit. Their leaders did not know if they would stand and fight -- or break and run. This battle line of untried road builders held fast and stopped the massive Confederate assault.

Notes:

[1] Bessie Brazee's Album:

Publisher:	Not marked
Dimensions:	4 ¼ X 7 inches
Covers:	Brown leather over boards. Gilt-stamped "AUTOGRAPHS" with classical frame on front cover
Pages:	Title Page "AUTOGRAPHS". White pages, gilt edged
First entry:	1877

[2] http://www.rootsweb.ancestry.com/~ilbiog/winnebago/cmbrazee.htm

[3] Goetzmann, William H. *Army Exploration in the American West, 1803-1863*. Yale University, New Haven, Connecticut, 1959..

[4] Fitch, John. *Annals of the Army of the Cumberland*. Lippincott, Philadelphia, 1864

[5] Wikipedia: The Battle of Stones River or Second Battle of Murfreesboro, was fought from December 31, 1862, to January 2, 1863, in Middle Tennessee.

[6] Wikipedia: James St. Clair Morton 1829 – 1864 biography.

[7] Ancestry.com: US Census 1880 Rockford, Winnebago County, Illinois. Christopher M. Brazee age 46, lawyer, Lydia L Brazee 43, Mary E. Brazee 10 (owner of the album), Kate L. Brazee 7, Caroline Brazee 5, Martin H Brazee 2

[8] Ancestry.com: US Census 1900.

[9] Ancestry.com: Mary Elizabeth Brazee. Birth: Apr 21, 1870, Rockford, IL. Death: Jan 29, 1947.

CHAPTER 13
THE LAST CAMPAIGN

Lillie Gilpin sought entries for her autograph album during the Civil War and after. Inscriptions were provided by two of her brothers, who served together in same Civil War Union regiment. A journal kept by the eighteen-year-old Ebenezer describes the last campaign of the War in which his older brother Thomas Gilpin was rewarded for bravery with a battlefield promotion. The brothers served under one of the War's "Boy Generals," officers who were promoted to command while still in their early twenties.

THE ALBUM

The words "PENSEZ A MOI" (Think of Me), embossed in gold on an orange paper insert, adorn the black leather cover of Lillie Gilpin's album[1]. The entries are mostly from Hanover and Jeffersonville, towns in southern Indiana, close to the Ohio River. Many were written in a five-year period starting in December 1861.

LILLIE GILPIN'S album 1861

Entries from after the year 1865 reveal that Lillie, who was denied entry into Hanover College[2] (the school accepted women students only from 1880), attended the Western Female Seminary[3] in Oxford, Ohio.

THE GILPIN FAMILY

Lillie's father, Samuel Nelson Gilpin[4] (1806-1886) grew up on family farms, first in Connecticut, and later, in New York State. The Gilpins, later still, moved to Ohio, where their residence was used as an early station on the Underground Railroad, providing shelter to runaway slaves fleeing to Canada. Samuel, his London-born wife Mary and their eight children finally settled in Indiana, choosing to live in Hanover, the college town close to the Ohio River that he selected for the education of his five sons.

THE CIVIL WAR: THE GILPIN MEN ENLIST

Samuel Gilpin Senior and three of his sons served in the Union Army. The father, although not an enlisted soldier, was employed by the army as a carpenter and helped to build the large hospital at Jeffersonville, just along the river from Hanover, opposite Louisville, Kentucky. Some of the entries in Lillie's album are signed from Jeffersonville.

The oldest Gilpin son, Tom, born in 1832, attended Hanover College, and by the age of eighteen was teaching in the county's rural schools. Seven years later, he read law with a Rushville, Indiana law firm and was admitted to the bar in 1856, becoming a prosecuting attorney for Rush and Decatur Counties. While still in Indiana he married, and the couple started a family. In April 1861, at the same time as the Civil War commenced, he moved his law practice to Bloomfield, in southwest Iowa, taking with him his wife and their son. He enlisted on August 17th, 1861 as a private with Company "E" of the 3rd Iowa Cavalry[5]. He was immediately made first sergeant, and two months later was promoted to second lieutenant, later achieving the rank of first lieutenant and then captain of his company.

A second Gilpin brother, Samuel J. enlisted on August 21st, 1861 as a corporal with the 3rd Indiana cavalry[6]; at the war's end he was discharged as a teamster.

At the beginning of the War, a third brother, fifteen year-old Ebenezer was still in school. In August 1862 the young man, just past his sixteenth birthday, chose to enlist with his oldest brother's regiment in Iowa and in the same company[7]. The younger man's writing skills were acknowledged by his assignment as a clerk, and he served the staff of the General commanding the army to which his regiment was attached. Years later, was later appointed to write the History of the regiment.

THE IOWA 3RD CAVALRY

In the months of August and September 1861, the regiment organized at Keokuk, Iowa, on the Mississippi River at the extreme southeast corner of the state. Early in 1862, the regiment saw service in southern Missouri, and distinguished itself at the Battle of Pea Ridge, Arkansas, an engagement which was crucial to keeping the state of Missouri in the Union. Men of the 3rd Iowa were later stationed in Arkansas until called on to participate in the siege of Vicksburg Mississippi, in May through July 1863; this action yielded control of the Mississippi River to the Union Forces for the rest of the conflict. The regiment continued to see service in Arkansas and Mississippi during 1863 and through 1864.

WILSON'S RAID

In March 1865, the 3rd Iowa joined other regiments to form the largest cavalry force deployed during the War. Brigadier General James H. Wilson was ordered to lead a raid to destroy the arsenal and munitions factories at Selma, Alabama. Selma was one of the few military bases left in Confederate hands at that stage of the war, with a naval foundry, gun manufacturing factory, a powder mill, and warehouses all still functioning.

Three divisions assembled, in the far Northwest corner of the state, ready to strike southward to Selma two hundred miles away. One division was led by General Emory Upton[8], of the Third Iowa

Cavalry. Upton was one of the "Boy Generals," so described because they were appointed while in their twenties. The leading Confederate general opposing them was Nathan Bedford Forrest, with a cavalry force of two and a half thousand men.

THE LAST UNION CAMPAIGN

The story of the raid, which lasted two months, is told in the words of the young soldier clerk Ebenezer Gilpin, traveling with General Upton. Here are brief excerpts from his journal, which was reprinted in the *Journal of the U.S. Cavalry Association* in 1908[9].

THE LAST CAMPAIGN

A CAVALRYMAN'S JOURNAL.

BY

E. N. GILPIN,

THIRD IOWA CAVALRY.

Reprint from the JOURNAL OF THE U. S. CAVALRY ASSOCIATION.

Title page of *The Last Campaign: A Cavalryman's Journal*

THE JOURNAL OF EBENEZER GILPIN

Gilpin described the approach by the Union Cavalry to Alabama and encampment near Gravelly Springs, Alabama.

> *Three divisions of the Cavalry Corps have come by way of Memphis, Nashville and Chattanooga, and are encamped along the mountainside from Waterloo to Gravelly Springs, Alabama, in the extreme northwest corner of the State. — An army of cavalry.*

It looks strange to see an army of 25,000 encamped, and see no long lines of infantry white tents, and hear no beat of drums.

General James H. Wilson is in command. He is one of Grant's trusted generals; he intends a swift saber-thrust at the heart of the Confederacy.

General Upton, commanding the Fourth Division of the Cavalry Corps, has just been ordered here from the Army of the Potomac; he limps slightly from wounds received in the battle of Winchester, where he was brevetted major general for gallantry. At Gettysburg he commanded a brigade, at Spotsylvania a division of infantry and artillery. He has his spurs to win as a cavalry officer. He is a young man to be a general, not yet twenty-six. He is slightly above medium stature, keen-eyed, and carries himself as a soldier. His voice is low, usually, and rather pleasant to hear; speaks quickly when excited; when he gets angry he is quick as a flash.

General Emory Upton: One of the "Boy Generals"

Ebenezer mentioned his brother by his rank of captain, when describing crossing the Tennessee River at Chickasaw:

March 16th. Broke camp early and took up our march over the hills for Chickasaw, General Upton and his staff officers riding together at the head of the division. Captain Gilpin, aide-de-camp, lithe, alert, riding at the General's side, waiting instructions as to the crossing.

Captain Gilpin and I started off to make the "grand rounds," visiting the pickets, seeing that every sentinel was at his post and the guards on duty. There is a fascination about the call "halt!" in the darkness, and the order to dismount and advance with the countersign. There is always the thought that some blundering Irishman will shoot you first and inquire for the countersign afterward. The boys are all wide awake.

SELMA, ALABAMA

The Union Cavalry charged the Confederates near Ebenezer Church, Alabama.

March 31st. We have marched forty-three miles to-day with the pack train and artillery, leaving the main body to come up later. General Upton was up till after midnight with the engineer who plotted the fortifications at Selma, with maps and papers spread out before them, studying and planning the downfall of the city

April 1st. Marched at daylight. Near Ebenezer Church, we met the enemy under General Forrest. The Confederates held the crest of a ridge, flanked by a deep miry creek, with artillery posted so as to sweep both roads. ... By a succession of impetuous charges we forced them from the field, dislodged them from the heights, and drove them helter skelter five miles past Maplesville Station. The road was strewn with guns, belts, cartridge boxes, coats and hats.

> *The day's events have been so many and so exciting, that I cannot record them. Captain Gilpin, aide-de-camp, advanced with a detachment of the Seventh Ohio Cavalry under orders to develop the enemy's line. It was bravely done at a great sacrifice, every man being killed or wounded under the converging fire. The genial captain came out on foot, with four or five bullet holes through his coat ; if he had not dodged one that went through his collar he would have staid with his horse — that was not good at dodging.*

On April 2nd, Ebenezer looked back at the destruction of the city of Selma:

> *April 2nd. Selma. We captured everything they had, and 3,000 prisoners. Forrest made his escape along- the river road, fleeing with his broken army. ... The Confederates running for life, jumping their horses over the bluffs into the river, our cavalrymen after them to the brink, cutting and slashing with their sabers. Soldiers yelling vengeance, for some of our men were shot from their saddles after entering the city; citizens scared, women and children screaming, excitement high everywhere. Of all the nights of my experience, this is most like the horrors of war — a captured city burning at night, a victorious army advancing, and a demoralized one retreating. The soldiers, overpowered by weariness, wrapped in their blankets, sunk to rest about the streets; the citizens, exhausted by excitement and fear, the cries of their children hushed at last, snatching a troubled sleep ; the wounded, lulled by opiates into forgetfulness of their amputated legs and arms; the dead, in their last sleep, with white faces upturned to the sky; for the passion, cruelty, bitterness and anguish of war, this Sunday night now nearly gone, will be remembered. If there is a merciful God in the heavens. He must be looking down upon this scene in pity.*
>
> *April 3rd. If we had laid siege to Selma, half the command would have been killed or wounded. As it was, we have lost less than four hundred.*

MARCHING TO GEORGIA

Ebenezer described General Wilson's decision to extend the raid and to march east to Georgia, and the approach to Columbus. That day General Lee had surrendered to Ulysses S. Grant at Appomattox, but the Union forces in the south had not yet learned of it, and General Wilson pushed on.

> *April 9th. General Wilson thinks the enemy badly crippled, and is determined to press on to Columbus, their stronghold in Georgia, and give the Confederacy a mortal wound.*
>
> *April 15th. From a hill, from which I could see every house in Columbus, every fort and earthwork, I watched the two armies maneuver until it was dark. Columbus is situated on the Chattahoochee River, where it flows through a beautiful plain at the foot of the mountain. Three bridges span the river; one foot bridge, below the town, crossing from Girard; an- other foot and railroad bridge, entering the main part of the city; and an old forsaken causeway a few miles above the town. The lower and upper bridges had been destroyed at our approach; only the main bridge remained.*
>
> *At 9:30 at night the Third Iowa was ordered forward at a charge, and away they went, yelling and shooting down upon the Confederates, who were not expecting an attack from that quarter or at night, and after a short resistance were driven from their first line back to the forts and in among the batteries. The charge was so impetuous, and as in the night friend and foe could not be told apart, the Confederates were panic-stricken and fled in disorder. Then our men charged over the bridge into the city. Columbus was ours!*
>
> *We ride and fight all day, hardly stopping long enough to eat and sleep. The day's occurrences must be jotted down, if at all, by the light of the camp fire. The fellows watch me writing, and want to know if I am "making my will." I am writing history, I*

tell them. "Sacred or profane?" asks the Major. It might be called profane, I reply.

Ebenezer commented that as much nine days after Lee's surrender, General Wilson had still not received the order to stop his advance.

April 24th. News of Lincoln's murder confirmed. It comes like a stunning blow. The soldiers loved him, and grieve for him as though they had lost a father.
News of peace unsatisfactory and doubtful. We are here to put down the Rebellion, if it takes ten years yet, the men say. Andersonville is so near that the war is a reality in-deed with us. Many of our men, who were prisoners and escaped, having been lying out in swamps for months, are coming in, starved and naked.

April 27th. Still no communication with the North, save through Confederate hands. Everything unsatisfactory.

April 28th. Everything is chaos here, the most extravagant rumors prevailing among the citizens; no reliable news of any kind. The suspense is almost unendurable. We are reduced to about quarter rations, and no coffee, and nobody can "soldier" without coffee. Our clothing is worn out, and we nearly all wear Confederate uniforms. It is time the war was over.

Northern papers received, with news of Lincoln's death, and the closing scenes of the war.

Evidently General Wilson was unaware that General Sherman had met Confederate general Joseph E. Johnston on April 17th at Bennett Place, North Carolina and again on April 26th when final terms were agreed, which ended the war for Confederate soldiers in North and South Carolina, Georgia and Florida.

ATLANTA IN RUINS

May 10th. Awoke this morning nearing Atlanta. Houses destroyed, farms laid waste, burnt ties and twisted rails plainly showed Sherman's onward march. ... Here and there are lonely patches of graves dotting the hillside.

May 11th. Atlanta is a ruin, not a business house standing, and not a dwelling, except a few marked by shot and shell — every tree and shrub about our camp scarred and cut into grotesque shapes by bullets. All the region is a battlefield ; lines of reddish-yellow clay earthworks, in every shape known to military science, stretch away as far as sight can reach, and torn into shapeless masses by the heavy guns.

The railroad was completely destroyed when Sherman was surrounding Atlanta. Blackened embers and beds of ashes show where the piles of railroad ties were fired, and the rails at white heat, twined around the trees. The little pines and oaks alongside are seared and blackened by the process, and many have three or more rails twisted around them.

Ebenezer was assigned to guard captured treasure; his brother Tom was ordered to move it safely to Governor Brownlow at Nashville, Tennessee.

Gold and silver is stored to the amount of half a million dollars, which the Confederates confiscated and we captured, besides five thousand dollars in gold from the Confederate treasure chest. I feel like a buccaneer or a bold brigand in here with this "unsunned heap" of treasure. Captain Gilpin has orders to take the State funds and deliver to Governor Brownlow, at Nashville. In barrels and boxes, it makes a load for two six-mule teams.

He quoted from a speech made by General Upton to the troops, summarizing the campaign from Chickasaw to Columbus, Georgia:

Leaving Chickasaw on the 22nd of March, as a new organization, and without status in the Cavalry Corps, you in one month traversed 600 miles, crossed six rivers, met and defeated the enemy at Montevallo, capturing 100 prisoners, routed Forrest, Buford and Roddy in their chosen position at Ebenezer Church, capturing two guns and three hundred prisoners, carried the works in your front at Selma, capturing thirteen guns, 1,100 prisoners, and five battle-flags, and finally crowned your success by a night assault upon the enemy's entrenchment at Columbus where you captured 1,500 prisoners, twenty-four guns, eight battle- flags, and vast munitions of war. You arrived at Macon, Georgia April 21st, having captured on your march 3,000 prisoners', thirty-nine pieces of artillery and thirteen battle- flags.

The soldier clerk reached the end of his story.

On my way back to headquarters the deserted fires were casting shadows that seemed to stalk like gigantic specters along the walls, over tumbled and charred roofs and fallen chimneys, and I realized that I had seen the end. The (Southern) cause was lost!

While on leave, Ebenezer Gilpin wrote in Lillie's album:

Jeffersonville, Indiana   March 8th, 1864
My dear sister
You have asked me to write a piece for your album - something "to remember me by" - you say. I know you would not forget me if I wrote nothing, for those old times we brothers and sisters passed so pleasantly together in our childhood's home <u>cannot be forgotten</u> - that "long ago" when leaves and flowers were brighter than they now are - when our life was one long holiday of pleasure and gladness. When we chased away the hours with fairy feet and thought not of the future save as one of uninterrupted happiness. Oh No - you cannot forget them- Alas they were <u>too full</u> of happiness

far _too bright_ to last. That happy band is now widely scattered. Each succeeding wave of time has dashed them farther and farther way from the old homestead. There is scarcely a possibility of our all meeting again for in this world of ours life is at best uncertain - that of a soldier still more so. We can but hope that _God_ in his providence will so order it that we may all gather again round our home altar safe from the many and various vicissitudes of this life without one missing. But if not here dear sister oh may we met in heaven our sweeter better home - never to part. Pray then that our hopes may meet with a _full fruition_.

Dear sister - please accept this little tribute as coming from the heart of your "soldier brother"-
                                            Eb.N. Gilpin

THOMAS C. GILPIN

For his bravery in the action at Ebenezer Church, Tom Gilpin received a battlefield promotion to Brevet Major[10].

Upon leaving the Army the army he returned to Iowa to pursue his law practice in the City of Winterset.

Tom Gilpin wrote in his sister's album:

> *Dear Sister Lillie*
> *I'll leave you my name and a line above it*
> *We will always love each other, won't we!*
> *Your brother*
> *Tom C. Gilpin   Winterset Iowa*

AN UNEXPECTED OUTCOME

One of the casualties of the Battle for Columbus, Georgia was a Confederate Cavalry lieutenant colonel, who, when the Union troops swept across the Chattahoochee Bridge, suffered a chest wound inflicted by Union cavalryman's sabre. Prior to the war, John Stith Pemberton[11] had been an Atlanta pharmacist. Treated with morphine for the persistent pain, he became addicted to the drug.

Pemberton experimented with a formula to relieve the addiction, and came up with a wine based on cocaine and Kola nuts. Forced by temperance legislation to try a non-alcoholic formula, he hit upon a carbonated drink that he called Coca-Cola.

Had General Wilson received word of Lee's surrender and had he not in the very last battle of the last campaign of the Civil War attacked Columbus, and had the Confederate pharmacist turned cavalry officer not suffered the painful wound at the Chattahoochee Bridge... the world might never have learned that "Things Go Better With Coke."

Notes:

[1] Lillie Gilpin's Album:
    Publisher: Leavitt & Allen, New York
    Dimensions: 9 ¾ X 8 inches
    Covers: Black leather over boards. Gilt-stamped "PENSEZ A MOI" in a circular recessed frame with orange background on front & back covers
    Pages: Title Page " PENSEZ A MOI" , Leavitt & Allen, NY Pastel pages, gilt edged, some with black white engravings
    First entry: 1861

[2] Hanover College, in rural Hanover Indiana, near the banks of the Ohio River, was founded in 1827, affiliated with the Presbyterian Church. It was officially an all-male college from its founding until 1880. Unofficially, women participated in the life of the college throughout the nineteenth century (attending college events, for instance). They attended classes as early as 1869. https://history.hanover.edu/courses/excerpts/121coeducation.html

[3] The Western Female Seminary was established in Oxford, Ohio in 1853 as a women's college, which sought to provide religious instruction and a college education similar to one offered to men in other institutions. It became the Western College for Women in 1904.
http://www.ohiohistorycentral.org/w/Western_College

[4] Ancestry.com: Summar42 family tree. Ebenezer Gilpin: born 1846. Details the Ten children of Samuel Nelson Gilpin (1806 – 1886) and Mary Gilpin.

[5] *The History of Madison County, Iowa*. Union Historical Company, Des Moines, Iowa 1879.
http://iagenweb.org/boards/madison/biographies/index.cgi?read=58869

[6] Ancestry.com: American Civil War Soldiers. Samuel Jr Gilpin enlisted Aug 22, 1861 in Company E, 3rd Iowa Cavalry Regiment.

[7] Ancestry.com: American civil War Soldiers. Ebenezer Gilpin enlisted Sep 1, 1862 as a Private in Company E, 3rd Iowa Cavalry Regiment. (He was 16 years, 2 months old).

[8] www.americancivilwarstory.com/battle-of-columbus.html "Raiders" photograph of General Emery Upton.

[9] Gilpin, E.N. *The Last Campaign: A Cavalryman's Journal*, Third Iowa Cavalry. Journal of the US Cavalry Association,.1908

[10] *A Memorial and Biographical Record of Iowa. T*he Lewis Publishing Company, Chicago, 1896.
http://iagenweb.org/boards/madison/biographies/index.cgi?read=58869

[11] www.americancivilwarstory.com/battle-of-columbus.html John Stith Pemberton, inventor of Coca Cola.

CHAPTER 14
A SOLDIER'S THIRD WAR

LIZZIE ALTON'S album 1866

In the autograph album kept by Lizzie Alton of Sanbornton Bridge, New Hampshire, is the signature of Charles Cressy, the man she married in 1869. He was one of three men from the same New Hampshire family who left home to fight for the Union cause in 1861. Only one returned alive from the Civil War. Cressy[1] was the son of one of the dead men and nephew to the other. After the war he studied for the Methodist ministry, and married the woman he met at the seminary. As a soldier and later as an Army chaplain, he served in not just one but three military conflicts..

THE CRESSY FAMILY

Charles' father, Joseph Presbury Cressy, was a blacksmith in Manchester, New Hampshire; his uncle Amos farmed, also in Manchester. The Cressys were descended from a family with a long history in America, present in New England since 1640, when a Richard Cressy arrived in Massachusetts from Kent, England. There had been Cressys in Britain since the year 1066 when William the Conqueror rewarded one of his knights from Crecy in Normandy with a Northumberland baronetcy.

ENLISTMENT

Within three days of President Lincoln's call for men on April 15th, 1861, Charles Amos Cressy enlisted in the 1st New Hampshire Volunteer Infantry; the young man was eighteen years old. Four months later, in September, his forty-nine-year-old father and his thirty-nine-year-old uncle Amos joined the 7th and 4th New Hampshire regiments,[2][3] respectively. That month Charles re-enlisted, this time in his uncle's regiment[4].

During the next two and a half years, the two regiments saw service together mostly in South Carolina and Florida. In May 1864, the were assigned to the Army of the James, for the attempt to take the fort at Drewry's Bluff, seven miles south of the Confederate capital Richmond, and the key to its defense. The Union Army landed from the James River and advanced to within three miles of the fort. However, Confederate infantry under General P.G.T. Beauregard counterattacked on May 16th. On this date, Charles Cressy was wounded and his uncle Amos was captured. Charles' father, Joseph Cressy lived to fight another day.

The New Hampshire 7th infantry remained involved in the siege of Richmond through 1864, and on October 1st of that year during the fighting near Richmond, Joseph Cressy was taken prisoner.

PRISONERS OF WAR

Charles Cressy's father and uncle were each confined in the appalling conditions of a Civil War prison camp.

When Belle Isle[5], in the James River opposite Richmond, became a Confederate prison it was intended to house no more than three thousand men, but its population swelled to double that. No barracks were erected; it was the only Confederate prison made up only of clusters of tents. Walt Whitman, when he saw men who had returned from Belle Isle, wrote, "Those little livid brown, ash-streaked, monkey-looking dwarves? - are they not really mummified, dwindled corpses?"

The Salisbury[6] North Carolina Confederate Prison compound was designed in 1861 for twenty-five hundred prisoners, and during the course of the War was forced to handle four times that many. Due to the Union Naval blockade, there was a shortage of medicine and medical supplies which resulted in terrible suffering of the prisoners and needless deaths. Throughout the South there was a shortage of food, and this prison was no exception. All the buildings were taken over for hospital use, and the men were forced to seek shelter that cold, wet winter of 1864 under the buildings, in overcrowded tents, and in burrows dug into the hard red soil. Burials before the overcrowding had been in coffins and in separate graves. The large number of men dying daily after October 1864 prompted to the initiation of a mass burial system. The bodies were collected daily and taken to the "dead house" to be counted and loaded onto a one-horse wagon. At 2 PM each day this wagon of the dead would be taken about a quarter mile to an abandoned cornfield where the men were buried. Eighteen trenches of approximately 240 feet each were eventually needed for burial of more than ten thousand Union soldiers.

Neither Joseph nor Amos Cressy survived their prison ordeals.

REV. CHARLES A. CRESSY

Charles Cressy recovered from his injuries, but was mustered out of the Union Army at Philadelphia in November 1864. After the War, Charles trained for the Methodist ministry in Sanbornton Bridge, New Hampshire, at the New Hampshire Conference Seminary[7] and Female College. While there he met his future wife, Lizzie, and inscribed in her autograph book lines from the poem "The Village Church" written by the Anglican churchman John William Cunningham (1780 – 1861). The style appealed perhaps to Charles the former soldier.

> *I love to know that not alone,*
> *I meet life's angry battle tide,*
> *But sainted myriads from their throne,*
> *Descend to combat at my side*

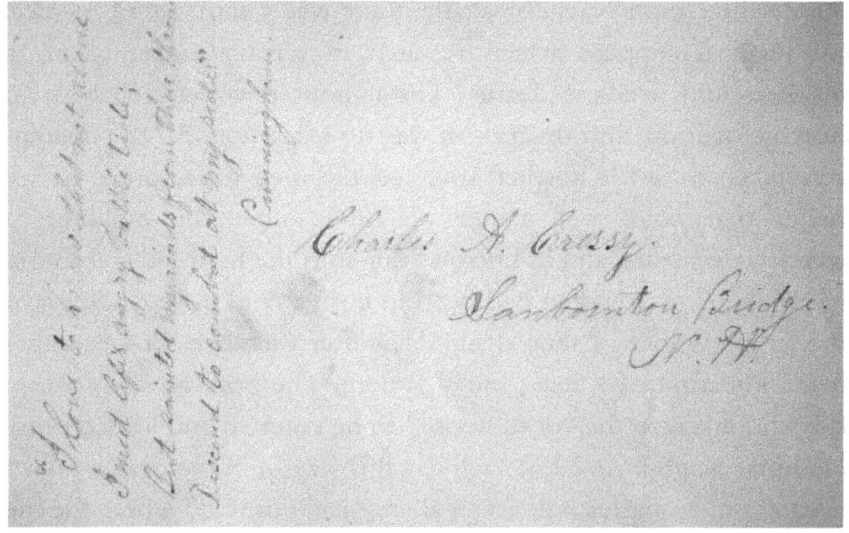

After Charles and Lizzie Alton were married in July 1869[8], Lizzie stamped the album with her married name[9].

Charles served in New Hampshire as a Methodist minister, sometimes traveling to preach in prisons and asylums in Brooklyn and New York , and in 1881, when he moved to Newport, Minnesota, to serve as a pastor.

A SOLDIER AGAIN – THE SPANISH AMERICAN WAR

In 1898, his quiet life as a minister was interrupted by events a thousand miles away. At 21:40 on February 15, 1898, the armored cruiser[10] USS Maine[11] sank in Havana Harbor, Cuba, after suffering a massive explosion.

USS MAINE in Havana Harbor 1898

The news of the blast and the deaths of 266 sailors stirred popular American opinion into demanding a swift belligerent response, and on April 25, Congress declared that a state of war between the U.S. and Spain existed. The conflict involved Spain's Pacific possessions as well as those close to the American mainland. Spain was already fighting an insurgency in the Philippines led by Emilio Aguinaldo[12], the ex-Mayor of the City of Cavite.

U.S. Commodore George Dewey had the Filipino leader transported from exile in Hong Kong to rally more Filipinos against the Spanish colonial government.

Emilio Aguinaldo 1898

By June, U.S. and Filipino forces had taken control of most of the islands, except for the walled city of Intramuros, the center of Manila. On June 12, Aguinaldo proclaimed the independence of the Philippines.

With the onset of hostilities between the United States and Spain in April 1898, President McKinley had requested volunteer troops from every state in the Union to support the U.S. Regular Army. In response to the President's call for soldiers, Minnesota mobilized its volunteer troops on April 29, 1898, with enough volunteers to form three regiments. When the troops of the Minnesota 13th Volunteer Infantry, were called for duty, Charles, at fifty-five years of age, was called to Army duty and was appointed to field rank as their chaplain[13] [14]. In charge of American forces was Brigadier General Arthur McArthur, father of the future General

Douglas McArthur, who would later also make history in the Philippines.

By June 26th, the 13th Minnesota had been equipped, had been sent on trains to San Francisco, had been trained briefly at Camp Merritt and boarded the troopship *City of Para* for the one-month voyage across the Pacific. For most of the men, it was the first time they ever encountered sea travel. A three-day stop in Hawaii was their only relief from the misery of heavy swells, seasickness and bad food. Delayed by a monsoon, they went ashore at the port city of Cavite in the Philippines on August 7th.

On August 13, with American commanders unaware that a cease-fire had been signed between Spain and the U.S. on the previous day, American forces captured the city of Manila from the Spanish in the Battle of Manila. The 13th Minnesota distinguished itself in the Battle, leading the advance. Twenty-three members of Cressy's regiment were killed or wounded. When hostilities with the Spanish ceased, the regiment was placed on policing duties.

The conclusion of the Spanish American War should have been the last experience of war for the Rev. Cressy, who was one of the oldest servicemen present.

THE THIRD WAR –PHILIPPINES vs AMERICA [15]

In the chronology of American wars, the conflict that occurred in the period between the Spanish American War and the First World War is seldom listed as a war. The Philippines–American war of 1899 – 1902 resulted in twice as many American casualties as its immediate predecessor.

The Battle of Manila which marked the end of fighting the Spanish also marked the end of Filipino-American collaboration, as the American action of preventing Filipino forces from entering the captured city was deeply resented by the Filipinos. When U.S. troops began to take the place of the Spanish in control of the country after the end of the war, Aguinaldo perceived that he had traded one

Colonial master for another. By February 1899, armed conflict had broken out between U.S. forces and the Filipinos. The 13th Minnesota found itself policing the City of Manila in the middle of another war, and was soon drawn into a role the fighting. Charles Cressy was experiencing his third war. In May, seven companies of the Minnesota regiment began a thirty-three-day mission to defeat the rebel forces. They covered 120 miles, captured twenty-eight towns, and destroyed enemy supplies. Then the rainy season swept into the Philippines, forcing an end to military operations. The Americans, Minnesotans included, complained about midsummer's boredom, monotony and heat. Orders sending the Minnesotans home came on July 13, 1899. A month later the men boarded the transport ship, *The Sheridan*. As the vessel pulled out of Manila Bay, the ship's band played "Home Sweet Home."

Fighting continued between American and Filipino forces, and Aguinaldo was captured in March 1901. The War dragged on until July 4, 1902, when President Theodore Roosevelt finally declared an end to the conflict.

AN OLD SOLDIER REFLECTS ON WAR

In September 1898 Cressy wrote about the war in the Philippines:

> *The natives [Filipinos] have some cause for their grievance toward the U.S. troops from their standpoint. They were waging warfare against the Spaniards. They had invested the city, cut off supplies from the country, stopped the water supply, and had actually driven the Spanish Army within their entrenchments and were holding them there when Dewey appeared upon the scene with his battleships. Now we prosecute a war on our own against the Spaniards, gain a victory, obtain possession of the city, and set the insurgents out[s].*

THE SOLDIER'S THIRD WAR 173

Charles Cressy, the old soldier, survivor of three wars, spent his remaining years in Minnesota, writing,[16] preaching, and attending regimental reunions. The Reverend Cressy died in 1917.

Notes to **THE SOLDIER'S THIRD WAR**

[1] Ancestry.com: Slattery genealogy. Charles Amos Cressy family tree.

[2] 7th New Hampshire Regiment Infantry History:
http://www.usgennet.org/usa/nh/topic/civilwar/nh7threg.htm

[3] 4th New Hampshire Regiment Infantry History:
http://www.civilwarindex.com/armynh/4th_nh_infantry.html

[4] Ancestry.com: US Civil War Soldier records and Profiles. Charles A Cressy, age 18, enlisted Apr 9, 1861 in Co. A, New Hampshire 4th Infantry Regiment. Mustered out Oct 5, 1864 at Philadelphia, PA.

[5] Belle Isle Prison:
http://www.encyclopediavirginia.org/Belle_Isle_Prison#

[6] Salisbury Confederate Prison Association:
http://www.salisburyprison.org/PrisonHistory.htm

[7] The New Hampshire Conference Seminary and Female College was founded in 1845 as a school for boys, and added female students in 1852.

[8] FamilySearch.org: Charles A Cressy married Lizzie M.C. Alton, Jul 21, 1869.

[9] Lizzie Alton's Album:

Publisher:	Unmarked. The styling of the word AUTOGRAPHS stamped on the front cover is identical to that on Pierre Hurlbut's album, which was published by Rufus Merrill & Son. Concord, NH
Dimensions:	4 1/4 X 7 inches
Covers:	Black leather over boards. Gilt-stamped "AUTOGRAPHS"
Pages:	Title Page none. Interior pages white with gilt edging
First entry:	1867

[10] Wikipedia: Spanish American War.

[11] Wikimedia Commons:
USS_Maine_ACR-1_in_Havana_harbor_before_explosion_1898

[12] Wikimedia Commons: from *War In The Philippines* published in 1899.

Photo of Emilio Aguilnado

[13] Minnesota 13th Volunteer Infantry. http://www.spanamwar.com/13mn.htm

[14] Ancestry.com: Minnesota Volunteers in the Spanish American War and the Philippine Insurrection. Charles A Cressy. 13th Unit, Field & Staff, rank Chaplain – Captain. Age 55.

[15] Wikipedia: Philippine - American War 1899 – 1902.

[16] Minnesota Historical Society: Charles A. Cressy: An Inventory of His papers.

CHAPTER 15
PROFESSOR GARDINER GOES TO WASHINGTON

Samuel Gardiner's signature
in the album of his daughter Ada.

Samuel Gardiner Jr. was a prolific inventor, who liked to style himself "Professor", as reflected in his signature on his daughter's album[1] page, although there seems to be no record of his affiliation with any academic institution.

During the Civil War his inventions were used to light the newly constructed Washington Capitol as a beacon of hope. His armaments innovation was decried as "too fiendish" for civilized use.

Gardiner's groundbreaking developments are recorded in the technology histories of the lighting, electric power and armaments industries. The historians missed, however, his front row presence at one of the most tragic and momentous events in American history.

ADA'S ALBUM

Ada Florence Gardiner, the owner of the album, lived with her adoptive parents, Samuel and his wife Lydia, in the family home in a fashionable location a few blocks from the U.S. Capitol building in Washington, D.C.

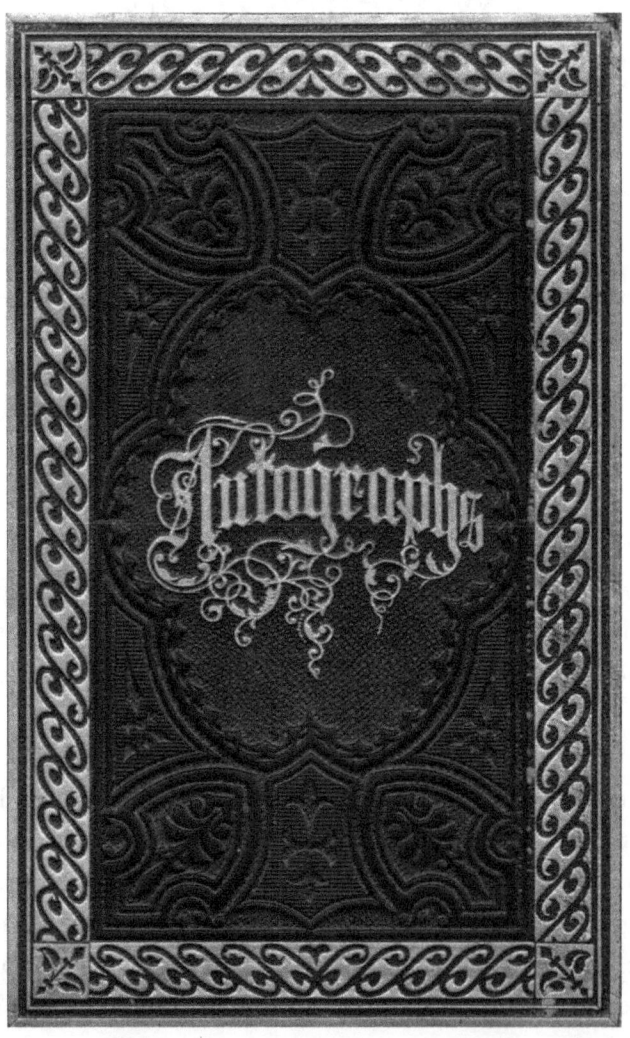

ADA GARDINER'S album 1878

When Ada was three years old the Gardiners moved from New York to Washington D.C. Ada grew up in a home that incorporated some of the inventor's innovations. To her and to the friends she brought home, it must have seemed as though there was something magical about the house. Two ivory knobs at the front door controlled a gas-lit chandelier in the front parlor. In the next room, a set of keys operated a second gas-lighted chandelier, and so on throughout the house. If any door or window was opened during the night, it would turn on lights throughout the residence. All of this was twenty years before Edison and his electric lighting.

In 1878[2], when Gardiner's elder daughter, Emma presented this autograph album to the young woman on New Year's Day, Ada was fourteen years old, Emma was thirty-five and their sister, Cornelia, was twenty-nine.

Selina Middleton, daughter of an English-born stone-cutter painted these flowers for Ada Gardiner's album.

The album includes entries from friends and from schoolmates at the brand-new Washington, D.C. High School, which graduated its first class in 1883[3]. More than sixty of Ada's requests for entries to her album were answered with poetry or artwork. Some were by the daughters or sons of people living close to the center of government, engaged in ordinary occupations. Many of the fathers were clerks in government departments, and others were in the professions.

This poem, signed only with initials, is from Charles Lamb's "In the Album of a Clergyman's Lady." It refers to the purpose of an album.

An Album is a garden not for show
Planted, but use; where wholesome herbs should grow
A cabinet of curious porcelain where
No fancy enters, but what's rich and rare
A chapel where mere ornamental things
Are pure as crowns of saints or angels' wings
Such, and so tender, should an album be;
And, lady, such I wish this book to be to thee.

M.N.L.   April 1883

SAMUEL GARDINER "ELECTRITIAN"

Samuel Gardiner Jr. was born in 1816[4] at Dalton, a rural/industrial community in the Massachusetts Berkshires. When he was six years old, his family moved to central New York State, where in the town of Onondaga he later met and married Lydia Huntingon, daughter of a successful and wealthy farmer.

By 1846 the couple had moved to Milwaukee, Wisconsin, where Samuel was in business as a watchmaker and jeweler. The census of 1850 records them with two children, Emma age six, and one year old Cornelia. Two years later they moved to New York City, where Samuel had the opportunity to apply himself to a series of inventions for extracting gold from ore. In the years 1853, 1854 and

1855 he was awarded patents for processes and machinery for washing, pulverizing and separating the ore.

Three years later he was immersed in the technical challenge that would dominate his creative abilities for the rest of his life[5]. The use of gas for lighting was widespread in American cities by the eighteen-forties, and the street gaslighter was a commonly seen figure. However, when gaslights were installed for large spaces, such as chandeliers in theaters, it was difficult and time consuming to light every gas jet by hand. In 1857 Gardiner built and installed an electrically operated system for controlling gas lighting in the Broadway Theatre in New York City, that involved modification of the chandeliers, the stringing of electrical wires and installation of a large battery. When completed, it took thirty seconds to turn on all the lights in the house, versus two men laboring for an hour to do the same task previously. In 1858 Gardiner was awarded his first patent for controlling and lighting gas lamps using electricity. It was the first in a long series of patents in this field spread over the next seventeen years.

For the census of 1860[6], Samuel described himself for the first time an "electrician." The title or occupation was at the time very new; the written record was misspelled by the census enumerator as "ELECTRITIAN."

Gardiner continued with more installations, including his own home, which he used as a showcase, to demonstrate his patented system for igniting gaslights using electricity. His approach to business was to contract for implementing systems that used his own inventions, and he was motivated to obtain intellectual property protection for his many ideas. During his career Samuel Gardiner was awarded 26 U.S. patents. One of his earliest inventions, patented in 1858, was an incandescent light using an electrical filament[7]. It had no vacuum and could not be operated continuously; its primary application was long-distance signaling.

His method of distributing electricity for control of a large number of gaslights also foreshadowed Edison's distribution of electricity for electric lighting twenty years later. Gardiner invented the first electric meter[8] in the history of the electricity supply industry, complete with dials to indicate units tens, and hundreds.

THE GARDINER EXPLOSIVE MUSKET SHELL

Early during the Civil War, Gardiner invented an explosive musket shell[9], and offered to supply it to the Federal Government at a price of thirty-five dollars per thousand. He described his invention as an "Improvement in Constructing Hollow Projectiles."

The fuzed bullet, patented in 1863 became the most controversial small arms projectile of the entire civil War. Designed to explode 1½ seconds after being fired, it would burst into fragments within an impact wound, severely lacerating the body of any human target it hit within a range of four hundred yards.

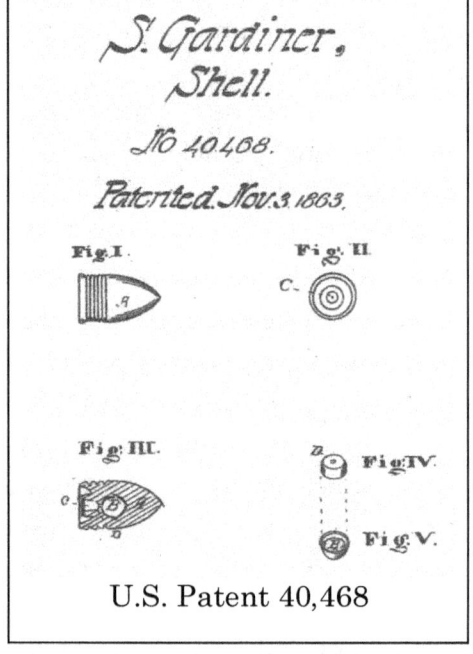

U.S. Patent 40,468

Consideration went all the way up the line to the President and 100,000 Gardiner shells were ordered; most were never used. Dislike by soldiers and claims by high-ranking officers that the projectile was "too fiendish" for civilized use, resulted in their withdrawal from service. General Ulysses S. Grant[10] complained, "Their use is barbarous because they produce increased suffering without any increased advantage to using them."

CIVIL WAR: THE CONSTRUCTION OF THE WASHINGTON CAPITOL

Gardiner's greatest opportunity to capitalize on his inventions emerged from the decision by the United States Congress to spend money on the Capitol buildings. In 1855 Congress appropriated money for a new dome for the Capitol building[11]. The North and South extensions that had started in 1851[12] rendered the appearance of the existing old dome disproportionately small in relation to the rest of the building.

Pre-1850 U.S. CAPITOL
(Wikimedia Commons)

A new design was selected, intended to outclass the most magnificent domes of Europe. The Capitol would be America's only major iconic structure until the 1880s, when the statue of Liberty and the Washington monument were constructed. The work on the Capitol Dome, started in 1855, continued until 1866. During the Civil War, construction continued, symbolizing an enduring nation.

(Photo. on next page, "Section through Dome of the U.S. Capitol."
courtesy of Wikimedia Commons)

The structure consists of two cast iron domes, one inside the other. Suspended 180 feet above the rotunda floor, between the two domes is a canopy, visible through an opening in the inner dome[13].

The Italian-American artist, Constantino Brumidi, was retained to paint on the canopy a fresco, called the Apotheosis of Washington. Measuring 4464 square feet, it shows the first president ascending into heaven, flanked by female figures representing Liberty and Victory. Six groups of figures surround the central figure, representing American achievements in War, Science, Marine, Commerce, Mechanics and Agriculture.

During daylight the fresco was illuminated through windows in the galleries supporting the dome. By night, however, some form of lighting was required. Chandeliers would have blocked the view from below. Lamps were needed around the perimeter, and long before the advent of electric lighting, gas lights had to be the solution. Lighting them one at a time, a hundred feet and more above the floor of the rotunda, was impractical.

THE PROFESSOR GOES TO WASHINGTON

The requests that was circulated for proposals for lighting the dome's interior, was the perfect opportunity for Samuel Gardiner to put forward his scheme for electrically controlled gas lighting. Gardiner had already installed a system for illumination of the Old Senate Chamber, a semicircular room with a half-dome roof that required 1500 gas burners. His proposal, based on his invention of 1857, combined electrical hot-wire ignition and solenoid operated gas cocks, all battery powered.

With the award of the contract, Gardiner threw himself into the project's design and implementation, and this required him to spend much of his time in Washington, away from his New York home. In April 1865, before the completion of the project, perhaps as a celebration of the news of Lee's surrender at the Appomattox courthouse, Gardiner took time off to attend a theatrical performance that would turn out to be the scene of an unexpected drama.

Completion of his lighting system required many more months of work. In January 1866, a demonstration of the illumination led to this flowery account[5] in *Scientific American*:

> *Entering the dark rotunda the visitors waiting "for the artificial light to dawn for the first time upon the splendid interior ... were amply rewarded for their journey on a stormy evening, the space above them showing like an immense vault through whose open mouth the heavens were visible, peopled with the fraternizing demi-gods of ancient and modern times.[14]"*

THE APOTHEOSIS OF WASHINGTON
(Wikimedia Commons)

A report of the Secretary of the Interior, dated July 31st, 1866, describing the installation included these words:

We take especial pleasure in commending the courage manifested by Mr. Gardiner in bringing his invention to the most crucical test which the country affords, by lighting up an interior of the area and height of the Capitol rotundo, dome, and tholus. [The tholus is the cylindrical structure of columns upon which stands the bronze statue Freedom.]

The gas pipe connections consist of circles of burners at 45, 80, and 165 feet from the floor of the rotundo, and are furnished with 300, 325, and 425 burners respectively. In addition to these, a cluster of 90 burners is placed in the tholus at a height of 264 feet from the floor, and being 60 feet above the crown of the dome, is, of course, invisible from the interior, but is a beautiful object viewed from the Capitol grounds, and visible at a distance of many miles.

The flow of gas at each tier, and in the tholus, is equalized by a regulator, and governed by a stop-cock, the latter being opened and closed by electromagnetic engines in their immediate vicinity, worked from the battery, the central brain of the apparatus from which ramifies the nervous fluid which vitalizes the motive agents and the illuminating coil of each of the 1,130 burners.

The battery occupies an eliptical room 45 by 36 feet, and consists of 200 glass jars of a depth and diameter of about 13 inches, containing two zinc plates 9 by 10 inches, weighing 6 pounds each, and an interposed carbon plate, all supported by suitable insulators in the acid bath. It is disposed on benches in concentric series in the room, and arranged in sections of 20 jars each, to be brought into service as required.

The connections consist of five miles of No. 10 copper wire, doubly wrapped with linen yarn, and, when necessary, encased in India-rubber tubing; this is securely laid in protecting pipes or through passages drilled through the walls, the return circuit from the engines and the burners being made through the gas pipes. The burners used have an indestructible lava tip, which acts as an insulator, and each is provided with an insulated coil of platinum wire, placed on one side of the orifice, so as not to interfere with the free exit of the gas, which is lighted by exposure to the red hot metal when the electric connexion is made.

An 1866 report[15] by the Commissioner of Public Building said:

The dome is lighted by electricity, the gas being turned on and lighted in about three minutes, by the manipulation of keys, arranged upon a dial-plate, and placed in one of the passages leading to the rotundo. The manufacturer of all the apparatus, and arrangement of the burners, wires &c., were by Mr. Samuel Gardiner, of the city of New York, under an invention patented by him; and the whole is one of the grandest triumphs of American art that can be well exhibited.

In the years following his triumphal completion of lighting of the Capitol dome, Gardiner put much energy into trying to get the Federal government to pay him what he considered was full payment for his services. He petitioned frequently and without success to be named "Electrician of the US Capitol."

Two years after he signed his daughter Ada's album, Samuel Gardiner died in Buffalo, New York in 1880, at the age of 64.

ADA GARDINER: THE LATER YEARS

Following Samuel's death, Ada's mother, Lydia Gardiner, and her unmarried daughter Cornelia moved to live in Lydia's birthplace Onondaga, New York. Mrs. Gardiner passed away there in 1908.

Ada[16] chose to live with her sister Emma and her husband Robert Minshall in Washington. After Robert passed away, Ada and Emma resided for a few years in D.C., and then moved to Cape Elizabeth, South of Portland Maine. The census for 1920, records the household consisting of Ada, who was then fifty-five years old, Emma, who was seventy-eight, and a private nurse they had retained. The census records for 1930 and 1940 show Ada and the nurse at the same address, a residence valued in 1930 at thirty thousand dollars. Ada died at the age of ninety-seven in South Portland, Maine in 1962[17].

A CHANCE DISCOVERY

This would be the end of the story, were it not for what was found by the subsequent owners of the house in South Portland, a Mr. & Mrs. John Holt, when they were going through personal papers that Ada had left behind[18]. They came across an original letter[19] from Samuel Gardiner to his wife, with his account of what happened on the evening of April 14th, 1865, the day he attended the theater. The letter was written on embossed lined stationary paper, 8x10 inches folded in half to form four leaves, fully covered in writing. (When the letter was auctioned in 2004, it was folded in thirds and was accompanied by a small envelope with the pencil inscription *John Holt - Gardiner letter*. The whole was enclosed in another larger envelope postmarked 1934 and addressed to "Miss Ada F. Gardiner, 8 Sea View Avenue, South Portland, Maine" with a return address from a Wall Street law firm.)

Evidently Gardiner, on one of his many visits from New York to supervise the ongoing installation of lighting in the Capitol Dome, had booked orchestra front row seats for the play "Our American Cousin", a farce in three acts. That same evening President Lincoln had also chosen to relax by attending a play; it would be his eighth and last visit to Ford's Theatre.

In his letter, Samuel addressed himself to "Maria", the middle name of his wife, Lydia, at their home in New York City:

You no doubt have received the particulars before my letter reaches you of the assassination of Pres. Lincoln. it was terrible for I saw it all. Mr Cook and myself Engaged front Seats for ourselves Mrs Foster and Miss Walcott and as the papers State, J Wilks Booth shot the President and jumped from the front of the Private Box, upon the stage, holding a large Boa knife about a foot in length. No one but a stage actor could have performed the deed with such coolness. As he landed on the stage he looked back to the private box with his Boa knife raised and said Virginia is avenged, and left the stage at its rear mounting a horse and Escaped. ...Such a scene I hope never to behold again. The ladies were in tears, some fainting ...

Like most of the members of the audience, Gardiner would not have been able to see, from his vantage point, the shooting of the President. His description however is consistent with contemporary accounts of Booth leaping to the stage from the presidential box holding the Bowie knife with which he had just stabbed Lincoln's aide Major Henry Rathbone.

Samuel Gardiner, the contributor to the Nation's technological progress through his inventions, was also present at one of the most dramatic events in American history

---

Notes:

[1] Ada Gardiner's Album:

Publisher:	Not marked
Dimensions:	8 X 5 inches
Covers:	Brown leather over boards. Gilt-stamped "AUTOGRAPHS" on front cover with geometric frame
Pages:	Title Page - none. White pages, gilt edged
First entry:	1878

[2] Ancestry.com: US Census 1880 Washington, D.C.

[3] Washington, DC, had no public High School prior to 1876.
http://www.theusgenweb.org/dcgenweb/history/school/washingtonhigh1883.shtml

[4] Ancestry.com: Family Peale tree. Samuel Gardiner, birth Jul 15, 1816 Dalton,

MA. Death Jan 12, 1880, Buffalo, NY.

[5] Schiffer, Michael Brian. Power Struggles: *Scientific Authority & the Creation of Practical Electricity before Edison.*(Discussion of Gardiner's career and achievements), MIT Press, 2008.

[6] Ancestry.com: United States Census 1860: Cape Elizabeth, Massachusetts.

[7] United States Patent 20,706: "Improved Electric Signal Light" Jun 29, 1858.

[8] United Sates Patent 132,569: "Improvement in Electro-Magnetic Meters" Issued Oct 29, 1872

[9] United States Patent 40,468: "Improvement in Constructing hollow Projectiles" issued Nov3, 1863

[10] http://theinventors.org/library/inventors/blgun.htm
Samuel Gardiner, Jr. received a U.S. Patent in 1863 on a "high explosive rifle bullet" in .54, .58, and .69 calibers. Fused to explode 1 1/4 seconds after firing, it ensured that any soldier hit by the projectile with a range of 400 yards faced the danger of the bullet exploding within the impact wound.

[11] https://www.aoc.gov/history-us-capitol-building

[12] Wikimedia Commons: "US Capitol 1846."

[13] Wikimedia Commons: "Section through the Capitol Dome."

[14] Wikimedia Commons: "Apotheosis of Washington" painting inside the Capitol Dome

[15] Papers Accompanying the Report of the Secretary of the Interior: Washington D.C. July 31, 1866. By Tal. P. Shaffner, Nicolas Pike and Edward H Knight..

[16] Ancestry.com: United States Census 1920: Washington, D.C.

[17] Maine Death Index: Ada F Gardiner died Jan 23, 1962, age 97, South Portland, Maine.

[18] *Palm Beach Daily News*: February 7, 1965. "Aged letter Recounts Lincoln Assassination."

[19] The letter was auctioned in 2004. (Live Auction World website details an auction held in 2004, LINCOLN ASSASSINATION LETTER).

CHAPTER 16
POOR BOY

Albums of the DULA sisters
MARY LAURA & ALMA, 1890 & 1892

In a small Appalachian Mountain community in North Carolina, two daughters of a Confederate States Army veteran grew up in a family that is identified with two notorious murders that occurred seven decades apart. The sisters' autograph albums[1] contain the family names of the principals in the killings. One of the incidents is memorialized in one of the best known of American folk songs.

THE AUTOGRAPH ALBUMS

Deep in Caldwell County, North Carolina is the hill country town of Kings Creek. Here in the late eighteen hundreds Mary Laura Dula and her sister Alma were given small and almost identical autograph albums. The cover of each little book has an embossed picture of two kittens looking over a fence, and in the background a picture of a sailboat on the ocean. The books are smaller than most albums, just four inches by three; many of the entries in each album were in pencil. The first entry in Mary's album is from 1890, when this young woman, who had attended school no later than fourth grade[2], was seventeen years old. One of the entries reads:

> "May your virtue ever shine
> Like the blossoms on a punkin vine."
>   L G. Dula   [this was from Mary's sister Lucy]

Mary's friend J.K. Coffey wrote:

> Miss Mary L. Dula 12.9.91
> Sailing down the stream of time
> in your little bark canoe
> may you have a pleasant life
> with just room around for two.
>   Your friend   J K Coffey

Inscription to MARY DULA from her friend J.K. Coffey

In Alma's book the first inscription is from 1892 when she was thirteen, and had just finished seventh grade, her last year in school. Her mother wrote:

"When over these lines you look
Remember it was yore (sic) mother
That wrote them in yore book."
Yore last friend owen (sic) earth
Laura E Dula.

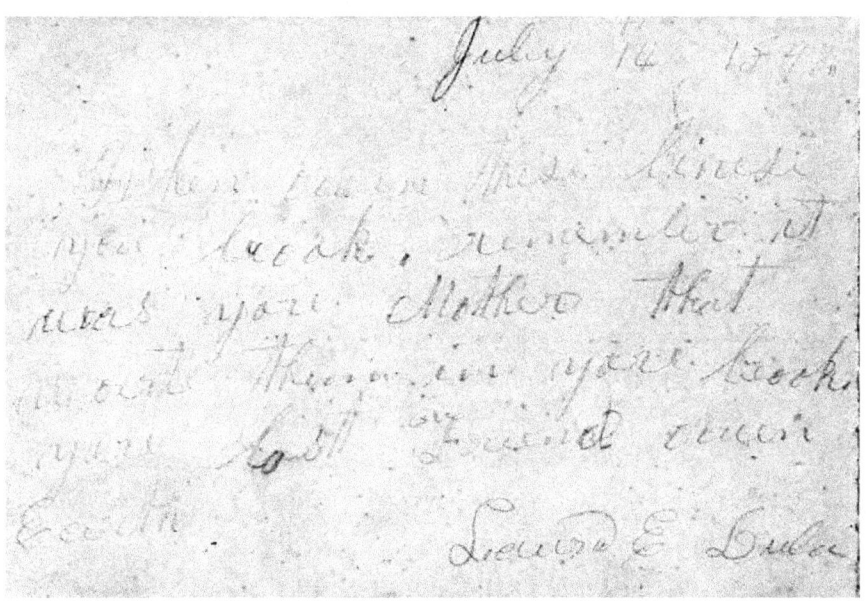

Laura Dula's message for her daughter Alma's album

Mary wrote for her sister Alma:

Sept 13, 1892
"Though many miles apart
Our future homes may prove to be
In the recess of your heart
Keep one kind thought for me."
Your sister Mary L. Dula

THE DULA FAMILY

In addition to Mary and Alma, the Dula family[3] included five more sisters and a brother Arthur, all children of farmer Thomas Wesley Dula, a Civil War Confederate Veteran, and his wife Laura.

Like many Appalachian children, Mary and Alma grew up in a region with a storytelling tradition, listening to tales that included regional heroic figures and events. One such local hero was the girls' own father.

Thomas Dula[4], at the age of thirty-one, already married with two children, together with his nineteen-year old brother James, enlisted in the Confederate States Army. The brothers were assigned to the "Caldwell Rough & Ready Boys" Company of the North Carolina 22nd Infantry Regiment.

Starting with nearly a thousand men, their regiment served in many of the major battles of the Civil War. It was with the Confederate Army from Seven Pines to Cold Harbor, fought at Chancellorsville and Gettysburg, and ended the war at Appomattox, Virginia in April 1865, when it surrendered[5] with 13 officers and just 67 men.

Thomas Wesley Dula and his brother James were both wounded in battle but each survived the War and returned to Caldwell County.

The girls grew up living with their parents at the farm. At the age of twenty-five, Mary married[6] a local boy six years younger than herself, John Wesley Coffey. Within a year the couple had one child, and two years later they were divorced, leaving Mary to bring up her son on her own; she moved back in with her parents. The divorced husband moved to neighboring Avery County and married again. Alma Dula lived at home until, after both parents had passed away; she eventually married at the age of forty-two.

THE COFFEY MURDER[7]

In the year 1936, when Mary was in her sixties, a story broke about a murder involving what would have been, to her, a familiar name. The Appalachian Mountains of North Carolina had become a favorite site of cabins for the well to do seeking respite from the southern summer heart, and a popular location for children's camps. James Hardy Coffey was an Avery County deputy sheriff responsible for assuring that the homes of absent owners were safe from thieves. He was shot and killed on Sunday, April 5th, leaving a wife and two children. The man convicted of the murder was the deputy's nephew, Ernest Reid Coffey, the son of the lawman's brother John Wesley Coffey, who at one time was married to the owner of one of the albums, Mary Dula..

The deputy had suspected the nephew of breaking into the summer camps around the county, and was scheduled to appear in Superior Court the next day to give testimony regarding the burglaries. On the night of his death he completed his tour of duty and had just returned home when he was fatally wounded by a single shotgun blast through a window. Ernest Reid Coffey, and some of his pals were known troublemakers in the area and the circumstances of the day and evening of the murder made him the prime suspect. The nephew was tried and sentenced to death in the North Carolina gas chamber, but the then North Carolina governor commuted it to life. Many in the family believed that it was not Reid who killed James, but John, the ex-husband of Mary Dula.

THE MURDER OF LAURIE FOSTER

A widely-publicized homicide that occurred seventy years before the Coffey murder also haunted the Dula family. This episode centered on Thomas Caleb Dula, the younger namesake and first cousin of the father of the owners of the little autograph albums. The saga became the stuff of folk legend.

Thomas Caleb Dula was born in neighboring Wilkes County, the youngest of three brothers. He grew up to be tall and good looking, a popular fiddle player and a favorite of the local girls and of some of the grown women. When Thomas was only fourteen years old, a neighbor, Lotty Foster found the boy in bed with Ann, one her three daughters.

On March 15th, 1862, three months before his eighteenth birthday, Thomas joined the Confederate army, serving first as a private in the North Carolina 42nd Infantry Regiment[8], and later promoted to the rank of "Full Musician." His regiment[9] spent much of the war guarding Petersburg, Virginia. Before the War ended he was taken prisoner, but survived.

Upon his return from soldiering, Thomas took up again[10] with Ann, even though she had, in the interim, already married a neighbor farmer, James Melton. Dula's romantic activities were extensive and he became intimate with two of Ann's cousins, Laura and Pauline Foster, from one or other of whom he caught syphilis. Folklore suggests that Laura became pregnant shortly thereafter, and that she and Dula decided to elope. On the morning she was to meet him, on or about May 25, 1866, she quietly left her home and took off on her father's horse. She was never to be seen alive again.

While it is not known for certain what happened that day, many of the stories that have grown out of the folklore of the time implicate Ann Melton in some way. Some believe that Ann may have murdered Laura Foster because she was still in love with Dula and was jealous that Laura was marrying him. Others believed that perhaps Dula knew or suspected that Ann had murdered Foster, but because he still loved Ann he refused to implicate her after he was arrested and took the blame for the murder. Ultimately, it was Ann's word that led to the discovery of the girl's body, leading to further speculation as to her guilt. A cousin Pauline Foster testified that Ann had led her to the site of the grave one night to check that it was still well hidden. Both Dula and Ann Melton were tried for the crime.

Witnesses testified in court that Dula had made the incriminating statement that he was going to "do in" whoever gave him "the Pock". Testimony was given that Dula believed Laura had given him syphilis, which he had passed on to Ann. The local doctor testified that he had treated both Thomas and Ann for syphilis, as he did Pauline Foster, who actually seems to have been the first to have contracted the disease. Many believed that Dula may have caught it from Pauline Foster and passed it along to the other Foster women, but that he believed he caught it from Laura.

Whichever of the three killed her, Laura's death had been confirmed when decomposed body was found in a shallow grave. She had been stabbed once in the chest. The gruesome nature of the murder, and numerous rumors that circulated in the small backwoods town when she was killed, captured the public's attention, and led to the enduring notoriety of the crime.

The role of Dula in the slaying is unclear. After her disappearance and before her body was found, he fled when he was declared a suspect. For a time he worked under an assumed name across the state line in Tennessee, for a Colonel James Grayson. When he had enough money to buy a pair of boots, he took off again. Once Dula's identity was discovered, Grayson helped the Wilkes County posse bring him in.

THE TRIAL

After Dula was arrested, former North Carolina Governor Zebulon Vance represented him *pro bono* and maintained the accused's innocence of the charges. Dula was convicted and, although given a new trial on appeal, he was convicted again. On Dula's word, Ann Melton was acquitted of the killing. On the first of May 1868, nearly two years after the murder of his fiancé, Thomas Caleb Dula was taken to be hanged. As he stood on the gallows facing his death, he is reported to have said, "Gentlemen, do you see this hand? I didn't harm a hair on the girl's head."

THE LEGEND & THE SONG

The controversy surrounding the conviction and execution lingered for years. Shortly after Dula was hanged a Wilkes County farmer turned poet, Thomas C. Land[11] penned a ballad about the tragedy that is still sung in the Appalachians Mountains.

Tom Dula, Tom Dula,
Oh, hang your head and cry!
You killed poor Laurie Foster,
And now, you're bound to die.

This song, combined with the widespread publicity the trial received, reinforced Dula's place in the local legends. Just as Nashville's "The Grand Old Opera" is pronounced "Opry" in the local dialect, the name Dula is pronounced in North Carolina as "Dooley." In the 1930s and 40s, the song was adapted by folk singers, and in 1958 The Kingston Trio recorded the hit version, with the title "Tom Dooley."

Mary Laura was seventy-one years old[12] when she died in 1944; Alma passed away aged sixty-three in 1942.

Notes to **POOR BOY**

[1] Dula sisters' Albums:
- Publisher: Not marked
- Dimensions: 2 ¾ X 4 inches
- Covers: Maroon paper over boards. Blind-stamped "AUTOGRAPHS" on front cover with image of kitten
- Pages: Title Page none.
- White pages, yellowed with age
- First entry: 1890 / 1892

[2] Ancestry.com: US Census for 1940, Caldwell County, NC. Alma Dula Mitchell, highest grade completed seventh. Mary Coffey highest grade completed

fourth.

[3] Ancestry.com: Nova's legacy family tree. Thomas Wesley Dula birth Apr 1831 in Caldwell County, NC, death Feb 16, 1924 in King's Creek, North Carolina.

[4] Ancestry.com: U.S. Civil War Soldier records and profiles. Thomas W Dula, Caldwell County NC, enlisted as a private in Company A, North Carolina 22nd Infantry Mar 19, 1862, aged 30.

[5] The Civil War in North Carolina: 22nd Regiment North Carolina Infantry. http://www.researchonline.net/nccw/unit98.htm

[6] Ancestry.com: Oxford family tree. Mary Laura Dula married John Wesley Coffey Apr 14, 1898.

[7] www.findagrave.com: James Hardey Coffey. Birth Jan 1886, Caldwell County, NC. Death Apr 5, 1936, Avery County, NC. Tells the story of Coffey's murder.

[8] Ancestry.com: U.S. Civil War Soldier's records. Thomas C Dula, residence Wilkes County, NC, enlisted as a private in Company K, N Carolina 42nd Infantry Regt. Apr 24, 1862. Promoted to full musician Jan 30, 1864.

[9] Ancestry.com: American civil War Regiments. 42nd Infantry regiment, North Carolina: Battles Fought.

[10] Wikipedia: Thomas C. Dula (June 22, 1845 – Ma 1, 1868). The story of the former Confederate soldier who was tried, convicted and hanged for the murder of his fiancée, Laura Foster.

[11] Thomas Charles Land was born March 18, 1828 in Wilkes County, NC. ... "the murder of Laura Foster was thus immortalized by a local poet." http://www.americancivilwarforum.com/the-poet-thomas-c.-land-and-the-legend-of-tom-dooley-1350.html

[12] Ancestry.com: Oxford family tree. Mary Laura Dula, born Nov 1872, death Apr 20, 1944.

BIBLIOGRAPHY

HISTORICAL EVENTS

Anon. *A Memorial and Biographical Record of Iowa.* Lewis Publishing Co., Chicago, 1896.

Anon. *Cyclopaedia of American Biography.* vol. 4, D. Appleton & Co., New York, 1888.

Anon. *The History of Madison County, Iowa.* Union Historical Company, Des Moines, IA., 1879.

Benson, John Lossing. *The Pictorial Field Book of the Civil War in the United States of America.* vol.1, Belknap, 1874.

Beyer, Walter F. and Keydel, Oscar F. *Deeds of Valor: How America's Heroes Won the Medal of Honor.* Perrien–Keydel Co., 1901.

Clark, Walter. *North Carolina Regiments.* vol. 4, State of North Carolina, 1901.

Fitch, John. *Annals of the Army of the Cumberland.* Lippincott, Philadelphia, 1864.

Gilpin, E.N. "The Last Campaign: A Cavalryman's Journal." in *Third Iowa Cavalry Journal.* The U.S. Cavalry Association, 1908.

Goetzmann, William H. *Army Exploration in the American West, 1803-1863.* Yale University Press, 1959.

Jones, James B. (compiler). *Tennessee in the Civil War: Selected Contemporary Accounts of Military and Other Events.* McFarland, 2011.

Joslyn, Mauriel Phillips. *Immortal Captives*. White Mane Publishing Co., 1996.

Knight, James R. *The Battle of Pea Ridge: The Civil War Fight for the Ozarks*. The History Press, 2012.

Knight, Lucian L. *A Standard History of Georgia and Georgians*. Lewis Publishing Co. 1917.

Linton, Charles. (The story of the writing of 'Our National Ensign' under the influence of the spiritualist Mary Cunningham). In *The Healing of the Nations*. New York Society for the Diffusion of Spiritual Knowledge, 1855.

Locke, John. (English philosopher) *A New Method for Making Common-Place Books*. 1706.

MacElyea, Annabella Bunting. *The MacQueens of Queensdale*. Committee of Publication of the Clan McQueen, 1916.

Martz, Col. Dorilas Henry Lee. Chapter VII "Rockingham in the Civil War 1861 – 1865 - A History of the 10th Virginia Regiment, Volunteer Infantry." in *A History of Rockingham County VA*. Wayland, John Walter (editor), Ruebush – Elkins, Co. Dayton, VA.,1912.

McGinty, Brian. (The re-capture of the *S.J. Waring*.) in *The Rest I Will Kill*. W.W. Norton & Co. 2016

Murray, Major J. Ogden. *The Immortal Six Hundred: A Story of Cruelty to Confederate Prisoners*. The Eddy Press, Winchester VA.,1905.

Murtough, Peter. *Condensed history of the Great Yellow fever Epidemic of 1878*. S.C. Toof & Co., Memphis, TN., 1879.

Penrose G. *Red: White: and Blue badge, Pennsylvania Veteran Volunteers, a history of the 93rd Regiment Known as The Lebanon Infantry*. Aughinbaugh Press, Harrisburg, PA., 1911.

Schiffer, Michael Brian. *Scientific Authority & the Creation of Practical Electricity Before Edison.* MIT Press, 2008.

Stokes, Karen. *The Immortal 600 – Surviving Civil War Charleston and Savannah.* The History Press, 2012.

Taylor, J.C. & S.P. Hatfield, S.P. *History of the first Connecticut Artillery and of the Siege Trains of the Armies Operating against Richmond 1862-1865.* Case, Lockwood & Brainery, Hartford, CT., 1893.

ABOUT ALBUMS

Falk, Bonnie Hughes. *Forget Me Not: a Collection of Autograph Verses 1880s – 1980s.* The Croixside Press, Stillwater, MN.,1984.

Fowler, Alice S. *Autographs: Verses from Old autograph books from 1878 – 1909.* Crescent Publications, Los Angeles, CA., 1976.

Fowler, Alice S. *Autographs: Verses from New England Autograph Albums 1825 – 1925.* Pioneer Books, Conyngham, PA., 1990.

Gernes, Todd. "Recasting the Culture of Ephemera" in *Popular Literacy.* Ed. by John Trimbur. Univ. of Pittsburgh Press 2001.

Henderson, Mary Jane Reichert. *Forget Me Not: An Album of Memories.* Delaware County Historical Association, Delhi, NY., 2002.

Matthews, Samantha. "Psychological Crystal Palace? Late Victorian Confessions Albums" in *Book History*, Volume 3. Pennsylvania State University Press, 2000

McClinton, Katherine Morrison. pages 125 -134 in *Antiques of American Childhood.* Bramhall House, New York, 1970.

Nickson, M.A.E. *Early Autograph Albums in the British Museum.* Trustees of the British Museum, London, 1977.

Ockenga, Starr. *On Women & Friendship: A Collection of Victorian Keepsakes and Traditions.* Stewart, Tabori & Chang, New York, 1993.

Thornton, Tamara P. *Handwriting in America.* Yale Univ. Press, 1996.

Todd, John. *Index Rerum.* Bridgman & Childs, Northampton, MA., 1860.

Tucker, Susan; Ott, Katherine and Buckler, Patricia P. *The Scrapbook in American Life.* Temple University Press, 2006

Wolf, Edwin. *Gothic Windows to Peacocks - American Embossed Bindings 1825 – 1855.* The Library Company of Philadelphia, 1991

COLLECTIONS OF VERSES FOR AUTOGRAPH ALBUMS

Anon. *Dick's Original Album Verses & Acrostics.* Dick & Fitzgerald, New York, 1879.

Anon. *Selections for Autograph & Writing Albums.* E.G. Rideout, New York, 1879.

Anon. *Uncle Herbert's Speaker's & Album Verses.* J.A. Ruth & Co., Philadelphia & Chicago, 1886

Dewitt, A.T.B. *Dewitt's Selections for Album Writers.* Henry J. Wehman, New York, 1885

Hayward, J. Harry. *Gems of Love, Friendship, Sympathy and Truth, For The Album.* Rudd & Carleton, New York, 1861.

Hooper, Lucy (editor). *The Lady's Book of Flowers & Poetry.* J.C.Riker, New York, 1843

Lamb, Charles. *Album Verses with a Few Others.* Moxon, London, 1830.

Ogilvie, J.S. *Seven Hundred Album Verses.* J.S. Ogilvie Publishing Co. New York, 1884.

Ogilvie, J.S. *The Album Writer's Friend.* J.S. Ogilvie Publishing Co., New York, 1884

INDEX

A

Abatis, 143
Abingdon, VA, 81
Age of Confederate Independence, 59
Aguinaldo, Emilio, 170
Albemarle County, VA, 133
Album, 1838 Vernon Rhodes', 117
Album, 1839 Sarah Forster Dixon's, 89
Album, 1850 John Barclay Fassitt's, 53
Album, 1855 Martha Rowe's, 14
Album, 1856 Lydia Rise's, 105
Album, 1858 Ella McQueen's, 128
Album, 1859 Mollie Carter's, 140
Album, 1861 Lillie Glipin's, 163
Album, 1861 Pierre Hurlbut's, 24
Album, 1865 Monnie Milburn's, 34
Album, 1867 Lizzie Cressy's, 173
Album, 1872 Harriet Smith's, 62
Album, 1877 Bessie Brazee's, 148
Album, 1878 Ada Gardiner's, 188
Album, 1899 Maude King's, 74
Albums, 1890 / 1892 Dula sisters', 198
Alexandria, VA, vii, 25–33
Allin, Major Phil T., 86
Ancestry.com, vi
Andersonville, GA, 131
Apotheosis of Washington, 184
Appalachian Mountains, NC, 191
Appomattox, 21, 31, 139, 157, 183, 194
Arp, Bill, 61
Atlanta Constitution newspaper, 61
Aubrey, George, 62
Austin, TX, 5, 8, 9, 10, 12
Avery County, NC, 195

B

Baldknobbers, 65
Baldknobbers Jamboree, 73
Batesville, AR, 68
Bayly, Marcus, 31
Beauregard, General P.G.T., 166
Belle Isle prison, 167
Bennett Place, NC, 158
Bensell, George Frederick, 52
Berry, Henry, 87
Best, Rawlins Desha, 128
Bill Arp, 61
Birney, General, 42
Blackmar gambit, 113
Blackmar, Armand E., 113
Blair, Montgomery, 31
Blockade running ships, 122
Bloomfield, IA, 151
Booth, 188
Boy Generals, 153
Bragg, General Braxton, 142
Branson, MO, 66–73
Brazee, Bessie, 141
Brazee, Christopher Martin, 141
Broadway Theatre, 179
Brown, John abolitionist, 134
Brownlow, Governor, 159
Brownsville, TX, 5, 9, 11, 12, 13, 14
Brua, Lt. Washington, 93
Brumidi, Constantino, 183
Buckner, Louise Berryman, 31
Buford, Cavalry General, 44

C

Cairo, IL, 78
Caldwell County, NC, 192
Caldwell Rough & Ready Boys, 194
Cameron, Simon, 19
Cape Elizabeth, ME, 186
Cape Fear River, 121
Capitol Dome, 181
Capitol, United States, 176
Carter, Mollie, 132
Carter, Richard & Nancy, 133
Cartersville, GA, 61
Cavite, 171
Cedar Mountain, 135
Cemetery Ridge, 45
Chamber pot, patented, 115
Chancellorsville, battle, 194
Chancellorsville, Battle, 135
Chantilly, 42
Chapultepek, 68
Charleston Harbor, 135
Chattahoochee Bridge, 163
Chattanooga, TN, 23, 67, 89, 145
Chickasaw, 155
Circlewood, 126
City of Hartford, 19
City of Para, 171
Civil War poetry, 93
Clay, Henry, 81
Coca-Cola, 162
Coffey, Ernest Reid, 195
Coffey, J K, 192
Coffey, James Hardy, 195
Coffey, John Wesley, 194
Cold Harbor, battle, 194
Columbus, GA battle, 162
Columbus, GA., 159, 160
Common Place Book, 107
Confederate Junior Reserves, 121
Confederate States Army, 1, 11, 28, 30, 61, 80, 121, 194
Confessions Album, 55
Connecticut, 14th Infantry, 21
Connecticut, 1st Heavy Artillery, 20
Connecticut, 4th Volunteers, 15, 18
Corse, General John, 56
Crescent City, 137
Cressy, Charles, 165
Cressy, Charles Amos, 166
Cressy, Richard, 166
Crinoline, 31, 32, 33
Crinoline and Quinine, 35
Cumberland, Army of the, 143, 148
Cummings & Hilliard, publisher, 117
Cunningham, Mary Jane, 96
Curtis, General Samuel R., 69
Curtis, W.W, poet, 94

D

Daily Memphis Avalanche, 87
Dalton, MA, 178
Davis, Confederate President Jefferson, 100, 121
Delaware River, 135
Dewey, Commodore George, 170
Dixon, Colonel LeonidasV., 79
Dixon, Henry St. John, 81
Dixon, Leila, 86
Drewry's Bluff, 124, 166
Dula, Alma, 192
Dula, Arthur, 194
Dula, Mary Laura, 192
Dula, Thomas Wesley, 194

E

East Tennessee Unionists, 99
Ebenezer Church, 155, 161
Edison, 177
Electritian, 179

F

Fair Oaks, VA, Battle, 92
Fassitt, John Barclay, v
Fitzgerald, Michael J., 104

INDEX

Floral Academy, 120
Florida, 2nd Cavalry Regiment, 41
Ford's Theatre, 187
Forrest, General Nathan Bedford, 153
Forster, Sarah Jane, 81
Fort Bidwell, 104
Fort Brown Flag, The newspaper, 11
Fort Delaware, 135
Fort Mahone, 23
Fort Pulaski, GA, 137
Fort Sumter, 61, 92
Fort Wagner, 135
Fort Wright, 101
Foster, Laura, 196
Foster, Lotty, 196
Foster, Pauline, 196
Franklin, Battle of, 146
Fredericksburg, 42
Freeman, Sergeant Henry, 147
French, Major William Foster, 121
French's Battalion of Junior Reserves, 123

G

Gallaher, Benjamin, 31, 32
Gardiner shells, 180
Gardiner, Ada Florence, 176
Gardiner, Cornelia, 177
Gardiner, Emma, 177
Gardiner, Samuel & Lydia, 176
Gas lighted chandelier, 177
Georgia Cracker, 61
Germantown, TN, 108
Gettysburg, *37–52*, 135, 194
    First Day, **44**
    The Third Day, **47**
Gilpin, Ebenezer, 152
Gilpin, Lillie, 150
Gilpin, Samuel J, 151
Gilpin, Samuel Nelson, 151
Grand Old Opera, 198
Granite State, 19
Grant, General Ulysses S., 69, 136, 180

Gravelly Springs, AL, 153
Grayson, Colonel James, 197

H

Hair token, 120
Hancock, General Winfield Scott, 138
Hanover College, IN, 150
Hanover Court House., 123
Harrisonburg, VA, 134
Hart, Minnie, 98
Harte, Bret, 60
Hartford, 1, 15, 17, 18
Harvard, 42
Hatfield, Samuel, vii
Hatfield, Samuel Proal, 15–23
Havana Harbor, Cuba, 169
Hayes & Zell, publisher, 128
Henry Rise, 92
Hilton Head, 137
Holmes, Lydia, 145
Holt & Williams, publisher, 62
Holt, Mr. & Mrs. John, 187
Houck, John W., 134
Hurlbut, Pierre, vii
Hurlbut, Pierre Proal, 15–23
Hurrah to the Clay, 82
Hutchins, Mary Octavia, 56

I

Illinois, 74th Volunteers, 143
Immortal Six Hundred, The, 131
Indiana, 151
Iowa 3rd Cavalry, 151

J

Jackson, Governor Claiborne, 69
Jackson, MS, 81
James, Army of the, 166
Jeffersonville, IN, 150, 160
Jerome, Aaron Brainard, 40, 44
Johnson, Senator Andrew, 99

Johnson's Division, 138

K

Keokuk, IA, 152
Kings Creek, NC, 192
Kirbyville, MO, 66

L

La Marseillaise, 113
Ladd, Luther C., 97
Land, Thomas C., 198
Leavitt & Allen, publisher, 34, 163
Ledbetter, Thomas Benson, 128
Lee, Eddie the drummer boy, 98
Lee, Robert E., 21, 42, 60, 69
Lincoln, President Abraham, 1, 17, 18, 24, 31, 32, 60, 61, 79, 92, 97, 136, 166, 187, 188
Linkhorn, Abe, 61
Little Round Top, 44
Locke, John, 111
Lockport, NY, 142
Lookout Mountain, 67
Louisville, KY, 151
Lyon, Brigadier General Nathaniel, 70

M

MacDonald, Flora, 126
Malvern Hill, 42
Manifest Destiny, 142
Manila, Battle of, 171
Mansfield, Camp, vii, 1, 15, 17, 18, 19
Martz, Colonel Dorilas Henry Lee, 131
Martz, Hiram, 134
Mass burials, 167
Massachusetts 6th Volunteers, 97
Maxton, NC, 120
McArthur, Brigadier General Arthur, 170
McCallum, Bella, 121, 125
McCallum, Lieut. Jas B, 124
McCulloch, Confederate Army General Ben, 70
McDonald, William Henry, 41
McDowell, Battle of, 135
McKinley, President, 170
McKintosh, General, 71
McQueen, Catherine, 127
McQueen, Colonel James, 125
McQueen, Donald, 127
McQueen, Donald "Donnie", 122
McQueen, Ella, 1, 119
McQueen, James Hugh, 126
McRae, Ann, 126
Meade, General George Gordon, 42
Medal of Honor, vii, 37, 48, 49
Melton, Ann, 196
Melton, James, 196
Memphis and Charleston Railroad, 112
Memphis Legion, militia, 78
Memphis, Battle, 78
Memphis, TN, 77
Merrill, Rufus - publisher, 24
Mexican War, 5, 68
Milburn J.P. & Co., 32
Milburn Pottery, 33
Milburn, "Monnie", 26–34
Milburn, Bendict C., 26, 27
Milburn, Ethelbert, 33
Milburn, James Clinton, 28, 31, 33
Milburn, John A., 28, 33
Milburn, Joseph Parker, 28, 32
Milburn, Monnie, vii
Milburn, Washington Clinton, 28
Milburn, William Lewis, 33
Miller, Samuel, 40
Milwaukee, WI, 178
Minshall, Robert, 186
Missionary Ridge, 67
Mississippi River Valley, 88
Missouri, 65–74, 152
Missouri, 24th Infantry, 68
Montezuma, 69
Morris Island, 135
Morrison, Lt. J.B., 123

INDEX

Morton, Captain James St. Clair, 143
Moss & Brother, publisher, 14, 105, 140
Murfreesboro, TN, 141
Murray, John O., 137
Musket, explosive shell, 180

N

Nashville, TN, 143, 159
Nassau, Bahamas, 122
National Military Parks, 74
New Orleans, LA, 113
New Zealand, 104
Newport, MN, 169
North Carolina, 1, 5, 21, 119, 120, 121, 126, 167, 191, 194, 195, 196, 197, 198
North Carolina 22nd Infantry Reg't, 194
North Carolina 42nd Infantry Reg't, 196
North Carolina 51st Reg't, 124
Northern mother, 94
Northern Virginia, Army of, 134

O

Old Senate Chamber, lighting, 183
Onondaga, NY, 178
Our American Cousin, 187
Ozark Mountains, 74

P

Patent, 23, 115, 179
Pea Patch Island, 135
Pea Ridge, Battle, 66, 71, 152
Pemberton, John Stith, 162
Pennsylvania 23rd Volunteers, 42
Pennsylvania 5th infantry, 92
Pennsylvania Railroad Company, 38
Petersburg, VA, 20, 23, 135, 196
Philadelphia City Troop, 42
Philadelphia Sketch Club, 52
Philippines, 170
Pickett's Charge, 47
Pickett's Division, 30

Pioneer Brigade, 143
Pock, 197
Polk, Major General Leonidas, 79
Postmaster General, 31
Powers & Weightman Co., 32
Price, Sterling, 70
Proclamation, Lincoln's, 18, 61, 79

Q

Queensdale homestead, 126
Quinine, vii, 32, 33
Quinine and Crinoline, 31

R

Railway Signals, 105
Rhodes, Katie, 108
Rhodes, Vernon, 108
Rhodes, Webster Nazer, 115
Richmond, Seven Days Battles, 135
Richmond, VA, 20, 21, 23, 31, 32, 122, 135, 166, 167
Riker, J.C. - publisher, 89
Rise, Adam, 93
Rise, George, 93
Rise, Lydia, 91
Rise, Samuel, 92
Robert the Bruce of Scotland, 125
Robeson County, NC, 120
Rockford, IL, 141
Rockingham County VA Female Institute, 132
Rockingham County, A History of, 138
Roosevelt, President Theodore, 172
Rosecrans, General, 143
Rosecrans, General William S., 142
Rowe, Martha, vii, 3, 5
Rushville, IN, 151
Ryan, Abram Joseph (poet), 84

S

Salem Heights, Rappahannock River, 92

Salisbury, NC prison, 167
San Francisco, 104
Sanbornton Bridge, NH, 168
Scarborough, Edwin B, 3, 5, 8, 9, 11, 12, 14
Scott, General Winfield, 69, 96
Secession, Texas, 10, 14
Second Manassas, Battle of, 135
Selma, AL, 152
Seven Pines, battle, 194
Shelby County, TN, 109
Shelly, Percy Bysshe, 113
Sheridan, The, 172
Sherman, General William Tecumseh, 56, 128, 136
Sherman's March to the Sea, 145
Signal Corps, 21, 41
Skye, Isle of, 126
Slave trade, 30
Smith, Charles Henry "Bill Arp", **61**
Smith, Harriet, 55–62
Smith, Hugh, 28
Southron, 114
Soutter Maitland, 40
Spanish American War, 171
Spotsylvania Courthouse, Battle, 135
Springfield, IL, 68
Springfield, MO, 68
Sprinkel, Charles A., 134
Sprinkel, Williette, 133
Sprunt, Alex, 122
St. Mary's, Raleigh N.C., 120
Stanton, Edwin M., 137
Stokes, Captain James, 144
Stones River National Battlefield, 146
Stones River, Battle of, 141
Stonewall Jackson, 68
Swann, John, 28
Syphilis, 196

T

Taney County, MO, 65
Taylor, Bayard, 96
Tennessee, 3rd Infantry Battalion, 80
Tennessee, secession, 78
Texas, vii, 3, 5, 9, 10, 11, 14, 62
Texas State Senator, 3
The Fayetteville (NC) Observer, 122
The Immortal 600, 137
Third Army Corp, 48
Tholus, 185
Tilghman, William, 103
Tom Dooley, 198
Topographical Engineers, Corps, 142
Trevino, 14
Trevino family, 13
Turner, Louisa Hipkins, 31

U

U.S. Cavalry Association, 153
Underground Railroad, 151
United Confederate Veterans, 138
Upton, General Emory, 152
USS Maine, 169

V

Vance, Governor Zebulon, 121, 197
Vanzandt, James, 65–73
Vern, Ella, 133
Vicksburg, MS, 81, 152
Virginia, 21, 40, 42, 47, 81, 88, 133, 134, 138, 139, 194, 196
Virginia 10th Infantry Regiment, 134
Virginia, 17th Infantry, 30

W

War Department, 19
Waring, S.J., Recapture, 103
Washington, D.C., 20
Washington, D.C. High School, 178
Webster County Regiment Home Guard Infantry, 70
Wesleyan Academy, 17

Wesleyan University, 15–23
West Jersey Collegiate School, 40
Western Female Seminary, Oxford, OH, 150
Weston, Major Eli, 71
White River Leader newspaper, 67
Whitman, Walt, 167
Whitney, Arthur P., 34
Whitney, Paul Clinton, 34
Wikipedia, vi
Wilkes Street Pottery, 28
Willard Banking, 47
Willard's Hotel, 28
Williamsburg, VA, 92
Wilmington, NC, 121, 122, 126

Wilson, Brigadier General James H., 152
Wilson's Creek, Battle, 65
Wilson's Raid, 152
Winchester, First Battle of, 135
Winterset, IA, 161
Wire road, 70
Wordsmiths, vi
Worsham, Colonel, 80
Wyoming Territory, 104

Y

Yancey, Hamilton, 58
Yellow Fever in 1878, 88

APPENDIX

More about autograph albums

THE ALBUMS

Autograph albums vary greatly in form and in the terminology used to describe them. In addition to "autograph albums", the terms include commonplace books, remembrancers and friendship albums. Closely related are scrapbooks, diaries and journals. It's not unusual to find elements of several of these categories in the pages of an album. The common thread is content that is primarily handwritten, and that was assembled by or for the owner. Academics sometimes use the expression "assembled books."

The earliest of the albums from which stories are drawn for this book date from the eighteen-thirties when the custom of writing one's own notes in what was often called a commonplace book was evolving into requesting inscriptions from friends, schoolmates and relatives. The physical style of the booklets evolved considerably during the nineteenth century, as did the nature of the written inscriptions and the quality of penmanship. Albums from the period before the American Civil War tend to have superior bindings and paper, with more elaborate and artistically decorated inscriptions. The locations and dates written in these albums correspond to the steady westward migration of population in America throughout the nineteenth century.

Illustrating these stories are examples of extraordinary penmanship, poetry and artwork. In the early eighteen hundreds, young ladies in finishing schools were encouraged to learn the art of painting in miniature.

A common reaction to examining an early autograph book is to be impressed by the superb quality of handwriting, the result of an education which employed formal systems of teaching penmanship, such as Copperplate and Spencerian Writing, and later the Palmer Method of instruction.

The quality and subject matter of poetic entries in albums varied enormously through the nineteenth century, declining in the later decades. Some verses are original; sometimes a copied entry is indicated by a phrase such as "selected for the album's owner". As albums became more and more popular in the eighteen-seventies, books were published providing examples of what was suggested to be "suitable verse." See page 204 for a list of such booklets.

No matter whether elegant verse or doggerel, meticulous script or child's pencil scrawl, miniature watercolors or crayon cartoon caricatures, the albums' contents convey a feeling of authenticity. At one time or another, each signed entry was the expression of how one particular individual, on a specific day and in a particular place responded to a request for "something for the Album". As such, the handwritten lines in autograph albums provide more precisely than almost any other antique artifacts, windows into American history.

As interesting as these books are, they have attracted relatively little attention in either popular or academic literature. See page 203 for a guide to what this author has found in the form of published books.

COLLECTING & EXPLORING OLD ALBUMS

Collecting these vintage books started for me by accident. Researching my own family history was temporarily stalled. A little booklet partly hidden on a shelf in an antique shop attracted my attention. The first page was decorated with a brightly colored lithograph of seashells and coral, with the single word "ALBUM." The handwriting throughout the album was beautiful, with inscriptions dedicated to the album's owner by friends and relatives.

Here was the opportunity to use familiar family history tools to explore someone else's genealogy. A name and a date and a place were all that were necessary to commence. I purchased the album and started the process. The dates of the entries in the little book were in no particular sequence of dates, but when I re-ordered them chronologically, they told the story of a young woman before and after her wedding in rural Minnesota of the 1880s. Once I had acquired and examined a couple more of these little books, I was hooked on collecting and researching old autograph albums.

Mid-nineteenth-century autograph albums in the author's collection

I found irresistible the idea that that it was possible pinpoint the exact place and date when, a hundred or more years earlier, someone held in their hands an album and wrote a greeting and their own name. Many of the books yielded information and anecdotes about their original owners, the people who left messages, and the places and periods. The accumulation of books expanded and a remarkable variety of narratives of people's lives accrued, prompting the notion of preparing for publication one or more books through which to share these stories.

To the reader I offer the hope that you enjoy this way of connecting with people whose inscriptions in autograph albums provide windows to events and places in American history. To family historians I would suggest that this way of exploring the genealogy of other people can be a lot of fun!

STORIES FROM AUTOGRAPH ALBUMS

From fading lines on the pages of albums that once were used to gather written mementos of schoolmates, friends and relatives, emerge the names of individuals whose lives can be traced through historical records.

Remarkable stories emerge when genealogical research brings into focus an interesting person or family, or a connection to an historical event or movement. The dates and places mentioned in the albums that inspired this book cover more than a century of American history as pioneers pushed the nation's boundaries ever westward.

We see individuals doing the ordinary things of life, going to school, marrying, having children, and moving to new homes in faraway places. As they write their greetings we get a glimpse of how they see the world, and learn something of their dreams and aspirations. Many of the owners of these albums were young women, and the sentiments expressed in these books are typical of an age when young ladies used them for a record of friendship with others of their gender, and when young men were expected to impress the opposite gender with male wit and knowledge.

People had a preoccupation with mortality, and expressions of feelings about death and the hereafter are common in the early albums. In an age of religious sentiment, and before our world was shrunk by modern communications and travel, we hear expressions of concern and hope for people who may be departing, "never to be seen again in this life." Instances of an album's owner recording the death next to an inscription are not uncommon. Expressions of the grief of a wife or husband for a dead spouse are all too frequent.

The stories in the present volume were selected for their connections to the Civil War era. In preparation are volumes with stories related to more historical events, celebrated names, pioneer families, and early examples of education and employment in America.

The Author

Graham Stubbs was born and educated in England. In the 1960s he was recruited to work in the United States as an engineer. His professional career has encompassed research and design in the electronic communications field, and resulted in the award of multiple patents for inventions.

As a hobby he enjoys seeking out for study those categories of vintage objects which escape the attention of most other collectors. His interests range from antique tools to early autograph albums. He edits a quarterly newsletter for tool collectors, writes frequently for tool collectors' organizations and has compiled for publication two encyclopedic books. He is also an avid researcher of family history, his own and others ...

Graham and his wife Stephanie reside in San Diego County, California.

Questions, corrections, suggestions
and comments about this book:

Please visit us at
www.fromfadinglines.com

Front cover
The circular inset on the front cover is
from an album dating from 1860.

Back cover
The background to the text is taken from a civil war
soldier's inscription to a girl's autograph album.

www.ingramcontent.com/pod-product-compliance
Lightning Source LLC
Chambersburg PA
CBHW070142100426
42743CB00013B/2801